Seven Steps to
Creative Children's Dramatics

SEVEN STEPS TO

Creative Children's Dramatics

by

PAMELA PRINCE WALKER

 HILL AND WANG · NEW YORK

To My Husband

GEORGE

ACKNOWLEDGMENTS

The author wishes to express her most sincere appreciation to her teacher of drama, Madame Tamara Daykarhanova, Daykarhanova's School for the Stage, New York City, for the inspiration underlying each page of this book.

The author would also like to express her appreciation to Mrs. Frederick S. Allen, Music Department, Children's Rehabilitation Center, Rutland, Vermont; Mr. Joseph Anthony, Broadway Director; Miss Nan Crow, Director, Charlottesville Recreation Department, Charlottesville, Virginia; Miss Lizbeth Laughton, Speech Department, Smith College; and Mr. and Mrs. Leslie H. Prince, East Poultney, Vermont.

Contents

Contents

INTRODUCTION

Creative dramatic classes are easy and full of fun. They are not a difficult and serious business. It is only necessary for the teacher to have something definite to teach. The teacher who confronts her class with the words, "Well, go ahead, make up a scene," will not get very far. The children are justified in asking, "Show us how!" The seven lessons in this book will show her how. Each lesson takes approximately one hour. Each lesson is filled with exercises which she may use in exactly the way they are written to teach the principles of acting to children. Each exercise has been tested many times in the classroom and has proved itself successful in bringing forth the best creative efforts of the group. By the end of the seven lessons, the children will be making up scenes with ease, playing characters with abandon, and using their imaginations with assurance. Never again will they recite their lines in a singsong voice. They will be prepared to act in a real-live play with a real-live knowledge of what they are doing.

A children's play must follow certain rules in order to incite the interest and enthusiasm of the cast and the audience. The lines must be short and simple; something exciting must be happening at all times; humor and wit must be prevalent; characters must be clear-cut and extreme; the plot must be imaginative. Leave the subtleties and innuendoes to the adult playwright. Leave him the lengthy conversations around the tea table. Children like action—not words. They like big, bumptious, frolicsome characters—very cruel witches, very kind fairies, very haughty queens—and nothing less. Three such plays are included at the end of the seven lessons; the first two have been tested several times with children's groups and proven highly successful. *Around the World in Eighty Days* is an adaptation of the Jules Verne novel especially prepared for this book.

It is the author's fervent hope that the teacher who would like to teach creative dramatics, but who doesn't know where to start, will read this book once, carry it to class the next day—and start! If she keeps it open upon her desk, follows the simple exercises day by day, and concludes the semester with one of the plays at the end, the chances are all in her favor for enchantment and gaiety she never dreamed could exist in a classroom.

The Seven Steps

Concentration and the Five Senses

1. "Who has ever been so engrossed in a book, that when Mother has called 'It's time for dinner,' he hasn't even heard her?"

"I have," cry the children, "I do it all the time!"

2. "Who has been that lost in his arithmetic lesson?"

No response.

"No one?"

Laughter.

3. "But if we could concentrate that hard on our lessons, we'd finish them much more quickly, wouldn't we?"

"Yes," say a few children, rather weakly.

4. "It's fun to get lost in something we enjoy—like a good story. Why do you suppose it is important for an actor to be lost in his play when he is performing? Why should he be so concentrated on the play he can't even think about anything else?"

"Because," says someone, "if he is concentrating that hard he won't miss any of his lines."

5. "That's one very good reason. Here's another. Suppose he is playing a very old man, all bent over and crotchety—like this—and now suppose he isn't concentrating very hard, and pretty soon he forgets and begins to walk around straight and strong—like this. Will the people watching believe he is an old man any more?"

3

"No! No!"

"He has to keep concentrating to remember his lines *and* to keep in his character every minute, doesn't he? Do you think the actor who doesn't speak very much in his role has to concentrate as hard as the one with a long part?"

"No," says someone, thoughtfully.

"No? When you go to a play, do you ever watch the people in the background, or an actor who is listening at the side of the stage—or do you always look at the person who is speaking?"

"I watch everyone on the stage, not just the big parts."

"Wouldn't it spoil the play if those people were not paying attention or not staying in character—if they were just daydreaming? Isn't it more exciting for you if they are excited and interested every minute, too? You see why an actor has to concentrate hard every minute to stay in character, to listen well and to remember his lines. He can't stop even for a moment, because the audience might not believe in the play any more.

CONCENTRATION ON A REAL OBJECT

"Let's see how hard we can concentrate if we try. Let's each take an object in the room and look at it, feel it, smell it—or whatever we want to do with it—but concentrate on it so hard we forget everything else. Even a pencil can be interesting if we really look at it. We can ask ourselves 'Who chewed this pencil?' 'What happened to the eraser?' 'What do those letters say?' 'To whom did it belong?' 'See how it shines in the light when I turn it this way.' 'See how smooth it feels.' Let's each take an object now and see how hard we can think about it. Forget the other children and what they have chosen. Your job is your object only."

The children walk about the room and choose objects.

Pretty soon there is a silence; each one is really concentrating on his object.

"No, Johnny, don't choose a book. It is too easy to lose oneself in a book. Take something more difficult—like that chair you are sitting on. You never know what you'll have to concentrate on in a play."

Now the silence lengthens. The children touch their objects, put them to their cheeks. They turn them about so they may catch the light. One or two may look about and giggle, but they soon stop when they see the others are too lost to pay them any attention. There is a long hush.

CONCENTRATION ON AN IMAGINARY OBJECT

"All right. Very good. Some of you were really interested in your objects, I could tell. Now let's move the objects away, out of the room if possible, and see how well we can imagine them. Pretend you are touching them again, and really seeing them, though they aren't here at all. Sometimes in a play we have to imagine things that aren't really there."

The children touch and see their imaginary objects.

"What color was yours, Suzie? How did it feel when you touched it?"

Again the room is in silence.

"Good. Very good indeed. You see how easy it is to concentrate if you try. From now on we will concentrate just as hard on all our acting exercises.

"Now let's concentrate on our first exercise. *The five senses.* Who knows what the five senses are?"

"I do, teacher. We had them in school. See, hear, touch, taste, and nose."

"And smell. That's right. Very good remembering. Now

why in the world would the actor on the stage use the five senses?"

"Because in a play you are always seeing something, or hearing something."

"Or tasting or touching or smelling something. That's right! And are all the things you're seeing or hearing really there on the stage?"

"No! Sometimes you have to pretend you're in a castle when you aren't."

"Right! Or smelling a paper flower which has no smell. Or hearing a clock chime, when it doesn't. Let's try some all together, and let's see if we can concentrate so hard we can really see or hear these things. Take your time now. It takes time to imagine clearly. Ready? (*Slowly:*) Through the window make-believe you see a beautiful sunset, all rosy and pink."

The children look out, enchanted.

Slowly, after a minute:

"Good. Now a thunderstorm is coming. See the big black cloud in the sky? There comes the first rain drop. See it?"

Cries of, "Yes, yes, there's another."

"Here it comes, harder and harder. It's really pouring now. See the rain splash on the window. (*After a long moment:*) Now the sky is clear again. It is night (*pause*)—the stars are beginning to twinkle. Do you see the moon? What kind of a moon do you see, Robin?"

"A baby moon with—with a little star on the end of it."

"Mine is big and round and orange. Like Halloween."

All eyes stare out the window. What miracle is in the making!

Slowly: "Now way off in the distance imagine a skyrocket going up, up, up in the night sky. When I tap my foot on the floor, like this, the rocket will go up."

Joey's face is a picture! At the tap of the foot, his eyes have lighted up, his mouth has fallen open. He draws his breath in sharply.

"What kind of a rocket did you see, Joey?"

"It zoomed straight like an arrow up, and exploded into a fountain—all purple and red and pink stars."

"What a lovely rocket! Joey is really concentrating well.

"We have used our sense of sight to imagine these changes outside the window; now let's work on the other four senses."

EXERCISES ON EACH OF THE OTHER SENSES *

The following exercises should be done slowly. Give time for the imagination to take hold, and time to erase one image completely before starting another. It is difficult to jump fast from the sweet smell of the rose to the strong odor of the garbage pail. Ask questions to encourage further imagining. Stress the importance of concentration during each exercise.

Hear
A clock in the next room strike six.

Distant music.

The faraway rumble of thunder.

A nearby clap of thunder.

The tramp, tramp of soldiers' feet and the big band in a passing parade come nearer and nearer, then go farther and farther away.

A distant train whistle at night.

A sudden gunshot.

Feel
A soft fur coat.

Velvet.

* Adapted from *First Steps in Acting* by Samuel Selden, pp. 238-39. Copyright, 1947, F. S. Crofts & Co., Inc. By permission of Appleton-Century-Crofts, Inc.

A piece of chewed bubble gum (held in the hand).

An ice cube (passed around class), followed by a pail of warm water.

A soft wind on a hilltop.

An icy winter gale.

The sun on the beach in summer.

Smell

(Pick it first, be sure you see it and feel it)—a rose.

(Lift the top off first)—a garbage pail.

An apple pie cooking in the oven.

A cow barn.

Gas being put in a car.

Taste

(Take a fork, or spoon, and concentrate on really holding it)—an apple pie.

Ice cream.

A spoonful of milk of magnesia.

Taffy candy.

Chocolate candy.

Coca-Cola.

EXERCISES ON THE FIVE SENSES COMBINED

The Birthday

It is the birthday of one of the children. He is kept outside the room and told to come in when the teacher indicates, as if he expects nothing and is just coming to class as usual. The rest have three minutes to prepare the surprise party with imaginary cake and candles to fix, presents to be wrapped, decorations to be nailed on the walls, paper hats to put on, etc. They must hurry or he will come in before they are finished, but they must be careful really to see and feel all the imaginary objects they use. They may talk as much as they wish. When he enters they will jump from their chosen hiding places and sing "Happy Birthday."

The Picnic

All the children are going on an imaginary picnic. Each carries his own contribution—the chicken, the pickles, etc. Some build a fire; others spread the cloth and food on the ground. How much can they see and hear? Can they feel the wind blowing? Is it salty? Are they sitting on soft grass or a hard rock? Is one bitten by a mosquito? Are there ants about? Is the sun warm? Can they see the ocean from where they sit, or only hear the breakers? Or perhaps they are near a stream in the forest. Is that a bird in the tree? What kind it is? They then eat the food, being sure they take the time to smell it, feel it in their hands, taste it, and swallow it. After a while one appointed child feels a rain drop, then another. There is a sudden downpour, and the children must pack all their food and rush to shelter. This exercise should be repeated until it takes a nice slow ten minutes. It takes time to imagine carefully.

"Today we learned to use our eyes, ears, and noses whether things are there or not, and we learned to concentrate hard when we act. Anything else we learned?"

"Yes," cries someone, "we learned to act a picnic. Was it neat!"

Physical Activities and Physical States

"Whenever we do something physically onstage, particularly when we use our hands, we call that something *physical activity* or *business*. People in real life are usually doing physical activities, even though they are talking to each other while they are busy. In the evening Papa is reading the paper, lighting his pipe, wiping his glasses, blowing his nose. Mama is washing the dishes, darning a sock, dusting the table. A little boy is bouncing a ball, taking off his sneakers, sharpening his pencil and preparing to do his homework. It does not look natural to see two actors stand onstage and talk to each other for a long time without moving about and doing some business. It is up to the actor to think of some activity his character might be doing if he finds he is just sitting or standing for a while in the play, even if it is no more than scratching himself. Let's see if you can think of twenty physical activities that might often be used onstage."

After the activities have been listed on the blackboard:

"Very good. Now each of you will take one of these activities and act it, while the rest of us guess which one you have chosen. What did we learn in the last lesson which will help us act these activities well?"

"We learned the five senses."

"We learned to concentrate hard on what we are doing."

"That's correct. We also learned to take our time and *really*

10

see and feel and smell. To be careful to put things down when we made believe we picked them up. To *believe* they were really there when they weren't. To *believe*. That's an important word for us from now on. *Believe*. Now let's try these activities and see how slowly and carefully we can act them so they will be easy to guess."

After the guessing game the teacher takes the children for a walk to a nearby place where much activity is going on—a drugstore, a busy garage, the school cafeteria. The children are told to keep their eyes open. They are not to talk; they are to observe. Each child is to choose one person and to observe his actions carefully. Upon returning to the classroom they will carefully reconstruct what they have seen, while the teacher walks among them, encouraging and suggesting. It is fun to invite a guest, perhaps another teacher, into the room and have her guess where the children have been as she watches them reconstruct the scene.

THE CLASS GOES TO WONDERLAND

The teacher puts a rubber ball on a table in front of the class.

"Now we will play a game in which we will use everything we have learned—concentration, belief, the five senses, and physical activities. This is Wonderland. We can go anywhere in the world from here by touching our magic ball. Anywhere at all! Think carefully now, where would you like to go! When you think of a good place, you may come and touch the magic ball and we'll all go there together. (*After a moment:*) Where would you like to go most of all, Mary?"

"To a carnival," says Mary, "and ride on the merry-go-round."

"All right, come and touch the ball, and when you touch it, everyone must imagine he is at a carnival. We will walk about the room slowly, and imagine all the gay things around us—the merry-go-round, the Ferris wheel, the shooting gallery, the candied apples to eat!"

Mary advances and shyly touches the ball. With many gasps from those who imagine they are riding the Ferris wheel, and contented sighs from those munching the apples, the children walk about the room and pretend the chairs and desks are the merry booths and rides at the carnival. Slowly, as imagination takes hold, they become more free with their actions and responses. Rapture shines on every face. The door to creativity has been opened.

Other places to go with the help of the magic ball (and more important, with the help of a few preliminary questions from the teacher to stir the imagination and excite the senses):

The cooky house in the depths of the dark, cool forest.

The beach, with huge ocean breakers to play in.

A ride on a sight-seeing bus through New York City.

SOME PHYSICAL STATES TO ACT

"We have worked on physical activities, now let's try some physical states. Often on the stage we must walk with a limp, or feel sleepy, or fall down and hurt ourselves. When we are feeling something physical we call it a *physical state*. Let me give you a few physical states first, then you think of some more and we will write them on the board next to the physical activities. A sprained ankle is a physical state. So is getting something in your eye. Or having a sliver in your finger —or a headache, or a nose cold."

The children think of more states until the list reaches twenty. Then they try some of them as they sit in their seats. They take their time and imagine the pain or discomfort clearly. After this, the teacher whispers a piece of business and a physical state to each child, and lets the others guess— both the activity and the state. The activity should be carefully chosen to enhance the discomfort of the state. For instance, a child who is acting a sprained ankle should not choose reading a book as his business. It is easy to read a book with a sprained ankle, and we would never guess he had a pain. On the other hand, if he chose to kick a football we would soon find out where the trouble lies.

Other ideas:

Reciting a poem with a bad cough.

Eating chocolate cake with an upset stomach.

Carrying a heavy load of schoolbooks with a sore back.

Playing the piano with a broken finger.

Jumping rope with a headache.

Serving tea with a bee buzzing nearer and nearer (finally the sting).

Trying to go to sleep with a mosquito buzzing about the ears.

Waiting for a bus in subzero weather.

They are lost in a blazing desert, and have been wandering for hours. They are very hot, tired, and thirsty. Suddenly they see a palm tree in the distance. A table and chairs stand in the shade of its leaves. As they approach it, they see a pitcher and glasses on the table. Some fear a mirage, but all move forward with renewed vigor. They reach the tree. Is it real? They touch it fearfully. Yes, it is! With a shout of joy they all rush for the glasses and the pitcher, which contains ice-cold lemonade. There is a dispute about who goes first, but there is plenty for everyone, and finally each child is taking long gulps of the refreshing beverage.

"Today we learned about physical activities and states. What is a physical activity?"

"*Doing* something."

"Correct. And a physical state?"

"Something that hurts."

"Well, pretty nearly. Although being sleepy doesn't hurt exactly, does it? And that's a physical state. Just being pleasantly warm—or cool—is a physical state, too. But most physical states do hurt, so you're just about right. Anything else we learned?"

"We learned to act carnivals. Was it cool!"

Colors (Emotional states) and Objectives

"Now we come to a very important part of the acting technique—*emotional states*. What do you imagine emotional states might be?"

"Crying and laughing and stuff like that?"

"That's right. Emotional states are just what they sound like. They are the emotions you feel at each moment in the play. It is important for the actor to know just what emotion he should be acting at any given moment in the play—and then to feel that emotion all the way down to his toes; to feel it inside, and not just pretend to feel it by making faces on the outside. We have a word for these emotional states. We call them *colors*. Why do you suppose we call them colors?"

"Because when you are crying you are blue?"

"Good. And what color is sunshiny happiness like?"

"Orange."

"Yellow."

"And anger?"

"Black."

"Red."

"Either black or red. Right. The actor uses his emotional states, or colors, to portray his character just as the artist uses the paints on his palette to make his picture. You see, I have left the physical states we named last time on the board. Let's put some emotional states next to them. Can you name some?"

"Crying," says someone.

15

"All right, let's call that sadness; for crying is what you *do,* isn't it, and sadness is what you *feel.*"

"Laughing."

"What shall we call laughing? Laughing is what you do. What do you feel when you laugh?"

"Happiness."

"Right. Any others?"

"Fear," says someone.

"Anger."

"Excitement."

"Irritation."

"Boredom."

"Love."

"Good. Now this list isn't as long as the others. And yet there are many, many emotional states. Do you think that could be because there are many kinds of happiness, sadness, and fear? A girl could feel pleasantly, peacefully happy lying on the beach in the sunlight, or joyously happy putting on her first evening dress. Both times she is happy, but one kind of happiness is entirely different from the other. What are some other kinds of happiness?"

"Silly happiness, like giggling in the movies."

"Right. Or how about the happiness that comes when we see our family after we have been away for a long time. And some kinds of fear?"

"Lying in bed late at night and hearing noises," says someone.

"Jumping into the deep water for the first time."

"Coming home with a bad report card."

"Good thinking! Those are three times we feel afraid, but how differently we are afraid each time. Now let's see if we can concentrate and really feel some of these colors. Pretend I am your teacher at school, and I have in my hand your report cards for the semester. Each of you is really worried (there is another emotion we haven't listed) about the grade you might receive in one of your subjects. I will pass them out now, but you mustn't open them until they are all distributed and I tell you to look. When you do look you will see a long list of A's. A for every subject, even for the one you had been worrying about. At the bottom of the card I have written a note which states, 'Johnnie or Sue is an excellent student.' How will you feel?"

Cries of joy at the very idea.

Pass the cards out slowly; build the suspense. Then give the signal for everyone to open his card. Repeat the exercise with each card a failure and the words "Johnnie or Sue is a poor student" at the bottom.

Other exercises on emotional states (to be repeated when necessary for more sincerity of feeling):

FEAR

The children enter a haunted house, dark and cobwebby. One child hides in the next room and makes ghost noises, while the others huddle together in terror. Finally the practical joker jumps from his hiding place, and everyone laughs in relief.

IRRITATION, MOUNTING TO ANGER

The children are trying to sleep when mosquitoes begin to buzz about their ears. Try as they will they cannot kill a single mosquito. Their irritation grows to anger and finally changes to relief as one by one they swat the mosquitoes.

EXCITEMENT AND ANTICIPATION

Girls: The girls are dressing in beautiful gowns for their first formal dance. They have only a few minutes before their dates will arrive.

Boys: The boys are dressing in a hurry for the Little League Champion baseball game.

BOREDOM

The children are waiting for someone to come. There is no book, piano, etc., in the room, and they are not allowed to converse with one another.

LOVE

Each child imagines he is fondling his favorite pet, doll, or Teddy bear.

APPRECIATION OF BEAUTY

The class is on a nature hike. They are standing on a high mountain and looking far out across the meadows and silver rivers. It is sunrise. A soft wind is blowing.

SYMPATHY

Choose a child who owns a dog. He is reading a book in his own living room when he hears the squeal of brakes outside. Then he hears the whines of a puppy. He rushes to the street. His dog is dead. The other children come along to take him to dramatic class. Upon seeing the situation, they do their best to comfort him and make him forget. This is a particularly meaningful exercise for children and should be repeated if it is not real and believable the first time. It brings out the best feelings of sympathy and helpfulness in the group, and many a little boy who has been troublesome in class will put forth his first sincere effort when the subject is this dear to him.

"Every time you have acted so far in class, you have had a goal—a desire to accomplish something. When you played the report-card scene your desire was to find out what grades the teacher had given you. When you worked on the color of anger your desire was to kill the mosquito. In the next exercise your goal was to dress in a hurry. What was your goal, or desire, in the last exercise?"

"To make Joey feel better about losing his dog."

"Correct! This desire to accomplish something when you act is called your *objective*. At each moment in the play the actor has an objective. It is important that he knows what objective he should be playing toward and then makes that objective a real desire within himself. There is never a time in the play when each character does not have a specific objective, just as in real life there is never a time when a person is without one, be it as simple as to eat a meal or tie a shoelace. What is your objective at this moment?"

"To understand what you are saying."

"That's right. Most of you are trying to learn at this moment. Although I see Johnnie's objective is to hand Suzie that note without my seeing him. And it appears Robin's objective is to go to sleep."

Laughter.

"Once the actor has decided what objective he should play, and made that objective a real desire within himself, he chooses the colors he will use to obtain this goal. Suppose Laura's objective is to convince Johnnie to go to the movies with her. She might use the color of excitement and anticipation first. 'What an exciting movie this is supposed to be,' she cries, enthusiastically. When this doesn't work she decides to change her color. Now she uses anger and threats. 'You'll never be my friend again unless you go to the movies with me,' she shouts, stamping her foot. Still Johnnie shakes his head no, so finally she tries sadness and tears, hoping this will bring Johnnie to pity her and succumb to her wishes.

"Now, let's try some objectives. I will give you an objective, and you may try as many colors as you wish to achieve it.

When one color doesn't work, change to another one. Don't play any one color too long, or we will become tired watching it. Two of you will act together. Decide first how your scene will end. Will one of you achieve your objective, or will you compromise? After trying a few colors bring your scene to this ending, so that it will not be too long to hold our attention.

"We have been talking about Johnnie and Laura, so let's give them the first exercise. Laura, your objective is to convince Johnnie to go to the movies with you, as we have said. Johnnie, yours is to do your homework for a very important test. What will your ending be?"

"I'll give in and go to the movies," Johnnie says.

"Very well. Keep changing your colors, Laura. And Johnnie, try as hard as you can to study, although Laura is bothering you. Don't forget your books, and just chat with her. Your objective is to study, and you must make yourself want that goal deep inside."

The children act the exercise. It is surprisingly natural for the first scene they have played, but they have had good preparation in concentration and belief. Perhaps it is too long, making it necessary for the teacher to call, "Let's bring it to an end now." Or perhaps it is so short we hardly had time to settle in our seats before it was over, making it necessary for the teacher to suggest repetition with Johnnie adhering more strongly to his objective and Laura playing her colors more fully before she changes them. After a few exercises, however, the children gain a sense of timing. They begin to judge just how long the audience will stay interested in one color and they end the scene at a point just before the audience will become restless.

Other objectives to try:

A.   *Child One:* A little girl has seen a beautiful sweater in a store window. Her objective is to convince her father to buy it for her.

Child Two: Her father has had an exhausting day at the office and has come home to find a pile of bills waiting for him on his desk. His objective is to read his paper and forget money for a while.

B. Child One: A mother has just found her best rug chewed to shreds by the family's new puppy. Her objective is to put an ad in the paper to sell the puppy.

Child Two: The little girl loves her puppy dearly. Her objective is to convince her mother to keep the dog.

C. Child One: One of the children has just found out who is to play the leading role in the dramatic club play. The teacher has asked her not to tell anyone. Her objective is to keep the secret, though she longs to confide it.

Child Two: Another member of the class hopes he (or she) will be chosen for the lead in the play. He has discovered the other child knows whom it will be. His objective is to find out the secret.

D. Child One: A child in the dramatic class is painting a chair for the scenery in the next play at teacher's request. This is his objective.

Child Two: Another member of the class enters. His objective is to take the chair home and decorate it with crepe paper—also at teacher's request. Teacher is not within reach, and an argument proceeds.

"You are advancing so very rapidly, I believe I will let you make up some of your own scenes."

Squeals of delight.

"Choose a partner. Decide your objectives. *Make them op-*

pose each other. If Laura had wanted Johnnie to go to the movies, and Johnnie had chosen for his objective 'to go to the movies' the scene would have been over before it ever started. Laura would have said, 'Want to go to a movie?' Johnnie would have answered, 'Good idea.' They would have left the room, and that would have been the end of that. Only because Johnnie wanted to do his homework, which *conflicted* with Laura's objective, did the scene have a chance to grow. Also decide upon your ending, just as you did before, so your scene will not be too long."

The children choose partners and are given five minutes to discuss their scenes with each other before they act. After each scene the class guesses the two objectives. With encouragement the scenes become very original—and sometimes quite funny, as was one with a shoe salesman trying numerous pairs of shoes on a fidgety customer. This was humorous enough, but the little actor chose a physical state as well—a bad head cold. He sniffled and sneezed, and grew increasingly miserable throughout the scene. Finally he lay down on the floor and fell sound asleep while the customer harangued him. Encourage the use of these physical states, physical activities, and other exercises the children have already had.

"Today we acted emotional states—or colors. What are they?"

"Feelings," says someone.

"Right. We also worked on objectives. What are objectives?"

"Wishes."

"Goals."

"Desires."

"That's right. Anything else we learned?"

"We learned to make up plays. Can we do more next time? Please?"

Animal Characters

"Who in here has seen a person who looks like an animal—perhaps a bulldog?"

"I have." "I have."

"Have you ever seen a big, tough person who walks around with his arms hanging loose and his head out—like this?"

"Yes." "Yes."

Laughter.

"What animal does he resemble?"

"An ape."

"A gorilla."

"Right. Perhaps you have seen a little, timid lady who fidgets with her pocketbook all the time—and tippy-toes about, like this, jumping at her own shadow. What animal does she resemble?"

"A mouse."

"A squirrel."

"Could be either a mouse or a squirrel. People are like animals, aren't they?"

"I knew someone once who waddled just like a duck. She really did."

Laughter.

"When an actor plays a character on the stage, he often decides what animal the character is like and then he talks and moves as if he were that animal. This is one very good approach to characterization. Up to now we have played ourselves, or our mothers or fathers. Now we will play some real

23

characters. First, let's try to act the animals as they really are. Everyone come out and kneel down on the floor. Don't look at anyone else during this exercise. Concentrate on your own character. That's your business, and nothing else. Take your time, as you did with your previous exercises. There is no hurry. Be sure you really *are* the animal—your movement, your actions, your feeling inside.

"First, be a cat. How does the cat move? How does she walk? Lie down? Sit? Eat? What are some habits she has? Does she scratch herself? Does she lick her paws?"

Other animals to act slowly and carefully:

> A playful cocker spaniel puppy.
> A pecking, nosy hen.
> A long, slow rattlesnake.
> A chest-pounding gorilla.
> A strutting, proud peacock.
> A roaring lion.
> A timid mouse.
> A waddling duck.
> A sleepy turtle.
> A fast-hopping rabbit.
> A big, lazy cow.

"Now each of you choose an animal to act and tell us which you have chosen."

"The lion," roars Johnnie.

"The puppy," yelps Joey.

"Fine. How does the lion feel toward the puppy?"

A ferocious roar from Johnnie.

"And the puppy toward the lion?"

With whines and yelps, Joey hides behind his chair.

"This is the *relationship* between the lion and the puppy. Now what is the relationship between Mary's proud peacock and Suzie's rattlesnake?"

Much hissing and fluttering of wings.

"Very well. All of you are going to make your way across the room to the trough on the other side where the food lies —the kind of food you like. Don't forget your relationship to the animals about you. Which animal will probably reach the trough with the least amount of trouble?"

"The lion." "The lion."

With much roaring and squealing the children start across the room. Cats are chasing mice. Rabbits are looking skeptically at cows, while cows are blinking sleepily back. Turtles are hiding under their shells. Mice are quivering in corners. When the exercise is over the children take their seats and try to catch their breath.

"Let's rest for a minute. Stay right in your seats for this next exercise. We will now be people who are *like* animals, instead of just plain animals. First, we will be people who are like cats. Just stay where you are, and let's hear each of you say the words, 'Hello, how are you?' as you imagine a cat would say them."

The words "Hello, how are you?" are repeated with the meow of the cat, the hiss of the snake, the moo of the cow, the quack of the duck, etc.

"Animals have very different voices, just as people have. Now choose an animal (it may or may not be one we have worked on), but don't tell anyone which one you have chosen.

"The room is now a train station. This table and chair constitute the ticket office. Laura, you come up and be the ticket seller. The standing lamp is the gum machine. That small stool is the weighing machine. This row of chairs is the waiting room.

"One by one you must come to the ticket office and purchase a ticket, then take your place in the waiting room to await your train. All the time you will be a person like the animal you have chosen. You will walk on your two legs, but you will walk as your animal would—playfully, stealthily, timidly, haughtily. When you ask for the ticket you will speak in the voice your animal would use. Use your hands to give the money to the ticket seller in the same way your animal would use his paws or claws. Stay in character even when you sit in the waiting room or work the machines. You will soon sense friends and enemies in those who are sitting near you in the train station. When the exercise is over we will all guess each other's animals, so observe the other children while you stay in character."

The above exercise may be repeated several times with each child playing a new animal.

"We will try some of our scenes again today. Choose your objectives to oppose each other, just as you did before. Choose your ending just as you did before. But this time also choose an animal character to play."

It may be necessary for the teacher to suggest one such improvisation to the children before they will feel they understand exactly what is expected of them. If so, the following improvisation is suggested:

Mary and Suzie enter. Mary is the mother, Suzie her little girl. They are in a drugstore. Mary's objective—to buy aspirin tablets. Suzie's—to buy a beautiful dolly she sees on the counter. The ending: Mary wins, and Suzie is transported, crying, from the store.

Mary, as the mother, could use a peacock for her animal character. She could be proud and haughty, walk with her nose high in the air, look at things around her through her monocle, and preen her new fur coat. Suzie, as the little girl, could use a playful puppy for her animal character. She could be full of deviltry and often overexcited. She could be awkward, and bounce into things on the counters, knocking them upon the floor. She could be whiny at times, but mostly good-natured and full of fun.

After this, the children continue with their own scenes, each couple deciding their objectives, their ending, and their animal characters before they act. These scenes are wonderful preparation for a play, for they include all the elements of a play—different characters in different situations. The children must now be encouraged to use their imaginations without fear of censure. Their characterizations should become increasingly bold and daring. Just as they have been encouraged in art class to paint in large, free, bright strokes, so must they be encouraged in dramatic class to act. Extreme characters are their meat. If they are portraying bullies, let them be *big* bullies; if they are supposed to act shy, let them be *very* shy. Save the delicate nuances for later years. Detailed, subtle characterizations are not meant for children. Teach them to open up and act in big, bold strokes—to throw their fears right out the window and "ham it up."

"Today we learned the first approach to characterization—people are like animals. Do you like to play animal characters?"

"I think animal characters are the most fun yet," says someone.

"Well, I'm glad of that, because until a play is written especially about you, you will always have to play a character when you act. Just keep playing them as clear and strong as you have today, and you will be fine actors."

Leading Centers and the Three Spheres

"In our last lesson we learned one approach to characterization. What was that approach?"

"Animal characters."

"Playing your character as if he were an animal. Right. Today we will learn two more approaches to characterization. The first is called *leading centers*. A leading center is a part of the body. It is the part of the body the actor chooses as the most important part for his character. From this part of his body the actor evolves his character. It is the center around which his character grows. It is his leading center.

"Suppose I choose my chin as my leading center. My chin is jutting forward—like this. I make it the most noticeable part of my body. Wherever I move, my chin goes first. I always remember to keep it jutting forward. What kind of a character does this make me?"

"A tough person," suggests someone.

"A prize fighter," says another.

"Very good. Now I make my voice match my tough character. I make it harsh and determined—like this. Next, I move heavily, perhaps angrily—like this. I evolve my character around my chin.

"Let's try some leading centers altogether. First, let's try using the top of our heads as our leading center. Everyone lower his chin and make the top of the head his lead. How

28

do you feel in this position, looking at the world from under your brow?"

"Like a mean person."

"Like a criminal."

"That's right. Distrustful, shy, maybe angry. Now try your shoulder. Lift one of your shoulders. Hunch it in front of you. Now how do you feel?"

"Shy and timid."

"Very good. Haven't you seen shy little girls and boys hide behind their shoulders—so—and giggle at the world? Now the chest! Straighten up and lift your chest high. How do you feel?"

"Brave and strong!"

"Like a soldier!"

"Like a bold, brave soldier! Good. And your nose. Try putting your nose out and sniffing about."

"A gossipy little old lady."

Laughter.

"That's right. Now turn your head so your ear is in front—so that it may become your leading center."

"A deaf person."

"Right. Now your stomach. Scrunch down in your chair. Relax your muscles. Protrude your tummy, so it becomes your leading center. How do you feel?"

"Sleepy."

"Lazy."

"Lazy and slovenly. Very well. There are many other leading centers. The lower lip is good for a pouting person; the upper lip might suggest stupidity. Consider the hands. If the hands are twisting and turning in front of the person—so—what character is suggested?"

"Nervous and fidgety."

"If the hands grope way in front—like this—what then?"

"Blind."

"If the hands are always stroking the chin, or touching the head thoughtfully—this way?"

"A teacher?"

"A teacher perhaps. Or a philosopher or professional person. At any rate, a person who thinks a great deal. If they are clenched—like this?"

"An angry person."

"Right. Now let's try each of these leading centers again and say the words 'Hello, how are you?' as the character would say them. These characters would have very different voices."

The exercise is repeated with the voice added.

"The classroom is now a photography studio. This chair is the camera. I will drape this tablecloth over it for the cloth under which the photographer ducks when he snaps the picture. Here next to the camera is a stick with an imaginary birdie for him to use. On the platform at the end of the room are two chairs where the people who pose may sit. Janie may play the photographer. She must be sure to take the name and address of the people who come to the studio, so she may know where to send their photographs, also to collect their money, and give them their change. She must pose them in interesting positions, and try to make them sit very still. I imagine this will be quite a problem, as some will want to argue with her, others will hide behind their shoulders and giggle, and so on. She will really have her hands full."

The children enter by ones, twos, or threes, as individuals, families, and so on, to have their pictures taken. As with the animal characters, each child is encouraged to play "big" and "free." Creative touches and original ideas, which should be quite numerous by now, are praised enthusiastically. The exercise may be repeated with each child playing a new leading center. It may also be repeated in a doctor's office with each one choosing a physical state to match his character.

"We come now to the third approach to characterization—
the three spheres. Look at this picture of a person I have
drawn on the board.

"You notice she has been divided into three parts. The
head is part number one; the chest is two; and the tummy
and legs are three. These three parts of the body are the three
spheres. Around these three spheres the actor may evolve his
character—just as he evolved it from one specific part, or leading center. Let us consider the first sphere—the head sphere:

"A first-sphere person centers his actions around his head;
that is, he uses his hands to make gestures around his face,
stroking his chin, smoothing his hair, scratching his head.
Of course, he may use his hands elsewhere, but they will return to the head most often. He uses the tips of his fingers
for these gestures and walks on his toes—like this. He is a
'lightweight' person, not necessarily in poundage, but 'lightweight' in feeling. Since he is a 'head-sphere' person, his ac-

tions originate in his mind, and not from his heart or lower down. Perhaps he is very intelligent and thoughtful—perhaps he is quite scatterbrained; both of these qualities suggest the mind, not the heart. He is apt to have a high voice which starts from his throat, not from his chest or tummy. Gracie Allen is a good example of a first-sphere actress with her dainty, finger-tip gestures and her high voice.

"The second-sphere, or 'heart-sphere' person centers his actions around his heart. He uses many gestures around his chest, clasping his hands to his heart, for instance. He uses his palms, rather than his finger tips, for these gestures. He walks on the ball of his foot, not the toes. His voice is lower than the first-sphere voice, and more 'heartfelt.' He is usually an emotional person; his emotions may or may not be sincere. Many actors are second-sphere people, as they must have this range of emotions in order to act. The person who cries 'Darling!' and pounds his chest—so—is a second-sphere person.

"The third-sphere person generally keeps his hands down by his sides, perhaps hanging loose, like the ape, perhaps on his hips, or tucked in his pockets. He uses the fist of his hand. He walks on the heels of his feet. He has a low, booming voice, which seems to start in his tummy. He is determined, willful, and often earthy. He is very much the opposite of the first-sphere person, and much more dogmatic and willful than the second. Marlon Brando is just such an actor.

"As you sit in your seats now, become a first-sphere person. Touch your toes lightly to the floor. Pick up your pencils daintily, using your finger tips. Touch your hair and your face lightly. Think 'high' and 'light.' Say 'Hello, how are you?' as a first-sphere person."

This exercise is repeated with the heart sphere, and with the heavy third sphere.

"The room is now a hat shop. Ladies' and men's hats are sold here. This long table makes a wonderful counter. Mary, you may be the saleslady. The rest of you choose a sphere to act. You must come one by one to the store to buy a hat—the kind of hat your character would want. We will guess what sphere you have played when you take your seat."

One by one the children perform. They are used to char-acter work by now and feel at home in the exercise, which is a simple one. It is easy to guess which sphere they are play-ing, for by this time they have learned to play extreme char-acters extremely. In the future it will be easy to guide them into dramatic characterizations by suggesting one of the three spheres, an animal, or a leading center to act.

Again the class period is concluded with the children choos-ing opposing objectives and improvising scenes with animal, leading-center, or three-sphere characterizations. From now on any spare time at the end of a class or rehearsal may be put to good use with these improvisations.

"Before we close today I would like you to take your pen-cils and copy the words I have written on the board. These are the first lines you have had to learn, and I expect you to come to class prepared to recite them next time. This half of the class will play Person One, and the rest of you Person Two."

The Words on the Blackboard *

Person One:	Hi.
Person Two:	Hello.
One:	Want a lemon drop?
Two:	Thanks. Don't mind if I do.
One:	You're looking well.
Two:	Think so? I can't say the same for you.
One:	Want another?

* This exercise, the working out of which is presented in the next chapter, was drawn from a similar exercise given by Joseph Anthony at Cecilwood Summer Theater, Fishkill, N. Y. Lines are adapted from Noel Coward's *Private Lives*, with permission of Doubleday & Co., Inc.

> *Two:*   No thank you.
>
> *One:*   Strange, isn't it? You here, and me—
>   this place—and all the rest of it.

"You will learn how we will act these lines next time. In the meantime don't worry about it. Just learn your part."

"Today we learned two other approaches to characterization. What were they?"

"Leading centers and the three spheres."

"What are leading centers?"

"Parts of the body to center characters around."

"That's a good description. And the three spheres?"

"Head, heart, and—um, feet."

"All right. What's the head sphere?"

In a squeaky, high voice: "People like this."

"And the heart sphere?"

Pounding the chest, in a "heartfelt" voice: "Darling! I'm so *sorry!*"

"And the third sphere?"

In a rough growl: "O.K., babe. This is toid sphere, see?"

Growling: "You got it, kiddo. Class is dismissed."

Transitions, Counterobjectives, Words and Feelings

"We have many times chosen objectives and tried to obtain them by the use of emotional states, or colors. Have you noticed that when you change from one color to another you must take your time? Have you noticed that it is hard to move from deep sadness to high joy very quickly? Doesn't it take a moment to realize what has happened and to change your feeling?"

Thoughtfully: "Sometimes it's slow, but sometimes it's pretty quick."

"Yes, sometimes it is pretty quick. But even then it takes a couple of seconds, doesn't it? This change from one color to another, whether it happens slowly or quickly, is called a *transition*. I will draw a line on the board—so. This line is your objective. This wavy line on top of it represents the colors you use to obtain it. Notice the colors go up and down, grow and diminish. They never stay the same. They are either rising or falling according to the circumstances. Imagine the part between each wave, or color, is the transition to the next color.

colors →
objective →

35

"Notice that sometimes your colors are big and sometimes small, just as they are when you are acting. But there is always a transition between two colors. Let us try to act two transitions—one very fast, one very slow.

"Imagine we are all sitting here quietly, reading books we enjoy. Take one of your books and read it. Feel peaceful and comfortable. When I tap my foot imagine a huge explosion in the room. Someone has shot a gun. The bullet has whizzed by your ear and just missed you. Fear will be your immediate color, and the transition from calmness will be very fast indeed."

The children open their books and begin to read. Although they have learned to concentrate, some of them will be busy waiting for the tap of the foot. It is hard to concentrate when we know a gun will be fired in a moment. Explain the need for belief in the moment, for living in the moment, in this exercise. If the children believe they are just peacefully reading and expecting nothing, the gunshot will come as a real surprise. When the teacher is certain that each child is reading, and not expecting the shot, she taps her foot loudly on the floor. The children jump from their seats and cry out in alarm.

"A very rapid transition, wasn't it? Now let's try a slow one. Johnnie is the postman. He will enter and give each of you a letter. When you hear his footsteps in the hall you will become very excited and happy, for you are expecting a letter from your best friend accepting your invitation to spend the summer together. Your excitement grows as you tear open the envelope, and slowly fades as you read the letter; it is a refusal. Be sure you imagine each word in the letter. By the time you finish reading you will have become very sad, but your transition will have come about slowly through the words you read, and not quickly as in the previous exercise."

The children act this exercise slowly and believably.

"From now on do not be afraid to take your time to make transitions in your acting, just as you take your time really to see, hear, or touch the things about you. Some actors rush through their play as if they were going to a fire. This is not lifelike. Never be afraid to take a pause onstage when you change from one color to another. The audience will be even more interested to hear what you will say next.

"I have one more exercise for you before we try the written words you have learned. This exercise will complete your training. After this, you must repeat and repeat what you have learned until you become very good—just as you must practice exercises you already know to perfect your piano-playing. This exercise concerns *counterobjectives*. A counterobjective is one objective on top of another. That sounds complicated, doesn't it?"

"Yes, ma'am! Phew!"

<u>counterobjective</u>

<u>objective</u>

"It isn't though. You'll see. Observe the line I have drawn on the board. It is your real objective. On top of it is another line. It is your counterobjective, the one you place on top, on the outside—the one you want people to believe is your real one. The best example I can use of counterobjectives is in the story "Snow White and the Seven Dwarfs." You remember the scene where the Queen dresses as an old peasant woman and comes to the dwarfs' cottage with a poisoned apple. What is her real objective?"

"To kill Snow White."

"Right. But what objective does she *pretend* is her real one?"

"To sell her apples."

"So selling her apples is her counterobjective; killing Snow White is her real one. I see Johnnie is trying to pass that note to Suzie again. He is looking at me with all kinds of interest while he does so, however. What is Johnnie's real objective?"

Laughter.

"To pass the note to Suzie."

"And his counterobjective?"

"To make you believe he is listening."

"Good. Thank you, Johnnie, for providing us with such a fine example. Now let us act a few counterobjectives. Make your real objective a real desire within you, just as you have before—just use the counter as a means of achieving your real goal."

EXERCISES ON COUNTEROBJECTIVES

A. Child One: A girl in boarding school sneaks into her friend's room to find a letter the friend has received from a boy. This is her real objective. When the friend arrives she uses a counterobjective of pretending she is looking for her misplaced arithmetic book.

Child Two: Arriving upon the scene, and quickly surmising the situation, the friend tries to steer the girl away from the top bureau drawer where she has hidden the letter. This is her real objective. Her counterobjective is to help her friend find the arithmetic book.

B. Child One: A boy is watching a movie with one of his friends. He holds in his hand a box of popcorn. His real objective is to keep the popcorn, which he wants for himself, away from his greedy friend. His counterobjective is innocently to watch the movie.

Child Two: The other boy tries in every way to sneak popcorn from his friend's box. This is his real objective, and he tries many devious methods of achieving it before he asks outright for the popcorn and is refused. His counterobjective is also to watch the movie.

C. *Child One:* Choosing an animal character (such as a tiger or rattlesnake) one child plays the part of the wicked Queen in "Snow White," whose objective and counterobjective have been previously mentioned.

Child Two: This child plays Snow White, also using an animal characterization (such as a gay little sparrow, or perhaps a lamb). She plays the simple objective of making the old lady comfortable and welcome.

"Have you learned the lines you copied from the blackboard last time?"

"Yes." "Yes." There is a spurt of enthusiasm.

As already mentioned, this is the first time real lines have been introduced.

"Will all the people who learned the role of Person Number One sit on this side of the room, and all those who learned Person Number Two sit over there?"

The children take positions on opposite sides of the room.

"Let's say these lines together loudly and clearly two or three times, until we are certain we all know them. The people who play the first person start, don't they?"

The children start.

"Hi."

"Hello." Etc.

"You have learned your parts very well indeed. Now we will act them. Let's have two volunteers for the first exercise."

Joey and Suzie raise their hands.

"Joey and Suzie may start. Come up here, please, and sit one behind the other on these two chairs. You are paddling a canoe in a raging current. The wind is whistling about you.

The waves are so high they are tossing water right into the canoe. Thunder is rolling. Lightning flashes. It is all you can do to keep the canoe from capsizing, and of course you must shout to be heard. When you shout "Hi" "Hello" you are naturally making a grim joke, as you have been paddling the canoe together for some time. It is an even grimmer one when you try to eat lemon drops. Take a moment to make sure you really believe in the situation before you speak to each other. Forget us—believe!"

The children shriek with laughter as Joey and Suzie struggle to keep the canoe afloat, and lose many lemon drops before one is finally delivered safely. At the line "Strange, isn't it? You here, and me—this place—and all the rest of it," Joey's face is such a picture of furious, panting resolution he nearly brings the house down.

"Who will volunteer for the next exercise?"

All hands fly up. All faces are alight with interest.

Other actions for the same lines:

Two people walk a tightrope toward each other, meet, carefully keep their balance as they speak the lines.

Two people are exploring a haunted house and meet in a dark room.

Two people run to a bomb shelter with bombs dropping all around. They speak when they are safe in the shelter.

Two people are hiding in a game of hide-and-seek.

Child One's objective: to go to sleep. Child Two's objective: to tease the other.

Characters to play, using the same lines:

Child One is a delicate, sweet bridal gown. Child Two, an avaricious octopus.

Child One, a beautiful peacock. Child Two, a galumphing clown.

Child One, a shaky bowl of Jello. Child Two, a porcupine (bent upon sticking Child One, of course).

Child One, a cat. Child Two, a mouse.

Child One, a mouse. Child Two, a cat.

Child One, uses the chest for his leading center. Child Two, a sleepy turtle.

Child One, the warm sun shining on the beach. Child Two, the north wind at night.

"Do you see how words change according to the feeling you are playing? How differently we say 'Hi' when we are shouting in the wind than we do when we are whispering in a game of hide-and-seek. How different was the delicate 'Hi' of the bridal gown from the greedy 'Hello' of the octopus, although both words mean the same thing when we just say them without feeling. That is why the actor must know his character, his objective, and his emotional state at all times. Without these, the words mean nothing.

"In review, now, what are transitions?"

"Changes."

"Changes from what to what?"

"From one color to another."

"Right. And counterobjectives?"

"Counterobjectives are two objectives, one on top of the other—like Snow White."

"All right. Anything else you learned?"

"Words don't mean anything."

"Words without feeling don't mean anything onstage. That's right. Anything else?"

"I learned to make believe I was a bridal gown."

"And me a peacock."

"And me a bowl of Jello."

"Did you like putting words and feelings together?"

"Yes, *ma'am!*"

Acting Games

"Today we are going to review what we have learned. Since this is the last class we will have before we start rehearsals for our play, I thought it would be fun to have a party; and so we will review our lessons by playing games instead of by acting exercises. The first game is called *statues,* and it will review our work with physical activities. Choose a partner, and come to the middle of the floor. Now take your partner's hands. When I say 'Go' you will swing each other round and round. When I say 'Stop' you will let go of your partner's hands and fall naturally into a position. Hold still in that position like a statue. Then I will ask each of you what physical activity you might be doing in that position. Ready? Go!"

OTHER GAMES WITH WHICH TO REVIEW PAST LESSONS

The Actor's Musical Chairs

Play a regular game of musical chairs. The person who is left out at the end of the game must think of a physical state and a physical activity to act for the rest of the class. The class guesses what state and activity he is acting. The game is repeated until only one person is left, as in regular musical chairs.

The Story Game

One person is chosen as the actor. He stands in front of the class. The teacher starts the story with one sentence about a character. The actor acts the sentence in pantomime. Each child in the class then adds one sentence to the story with the actor pantomiming it. The last person must finish the story. The game is repeated until each child has had a chance to be the actor. Some good sentences for the teacher to use as "starters":

"The old witch hurried out of her cooky house, cackled loudly, and jumped onto the broomstick."

"The haughty King held his nose high in the air as he paraded down the aisle."

"The little pixie peeked around the petunia, and giggled."

"The fairy princess danced gracefully about the glen on her toes."

"The old beggar held his hat out for pennies as he hobbled across the village square."

"The ghost floated into the graveyard at the stroke of midnight."

The Broomstick Game

Two broomsticks, two paper bags, crayons, and some old clothes or costumes are provided. The class is divided into two groups. Each group is given one broomstick, and one paper bag to tie on the end for a head. With the crayons they color a face, then tie and pin the clothes onto the stick, developing a broomstick character. When the two characters are finished the class makes up a short scene which might take place between them. Two people carry the large puppets about the room for the actions, while two others speak the words for the scene.

Charades

Each child draws the name of a book, movie, play, song, or slogan from a pile of such titles the teacher has written. He pantomimes the title, word by word, for the others to guess. He may not speak, but must pantomime the word so carefully the others will be able to guess it. The class may be divided into teams for this game with the teacher keeping time. The team which takes the least time to guess the title wins.

Twenty easy titles for children's charades:

"Snow White and the Seven Dwarfs"
"Smoke Kools"
"Little Red Riding Hood"
"Laughing on the Outside, Crying on the Inside"
"The Little Lame Prince"
"The King and I"
"The Man on the Flying Trapeze"
"Falling in Love with Love"
"The Old Woman Who Lived in the Shoe"
"Beautiful Dreamer"
"The King's Breakfast"
"So round, so firm, so fully packed"
"The Wind in the Willows"
"The Toy Tiger"
"The Turtle and the Hare"
"Old Man River"
"Rockabye Baby on the Tree Top"
"The Time of the Cuckoo"
"The Voice of the Turtle"
"The High and the Mighty"

A Poem To Be Read by the Teacher and Pantomimed by the Class

At the end of the class period the teacher may cast the following characters from the students for "Sleeping Beauty":

King	Jester	Sleeping Beauty
Queen	Elf	Old Nell
Maid	Three Fairies	Prince

Then she will read the following poem while each child must listen for his or her part and do exactly what is designated. Each child is encouraged to *move* and *feel* just as the character all the way through the poem.

SLEEPING BEAUTY *

SCENE 1

There once was a King who loved his money,
(King counts money.)
And a Queen whose nature was bright and sunny,
(Queen smiles, etc.)
The Queen had a Maid whose merry eyes glowed,
And the Maid loved a Fool who walked pigeon-toed.

The King was counting his money one day,
One merry day in the month of May,
When up jumped the Jester, up jumped the Maid,
And up jumped the Queen, looking afraid.

"I know you won't like this, darling," she said,
(Queen does not speak, but
looks worried and gestures.)
"But this morning guess what I found on the bed?
More money we now are obliged to spend
For a baby it now is our duty to tend."

"A baby!" the King cried, amazed and aghast,
"Now how will our income be able to last?
Where is it?" he howled, blowing his nose.
"I'll get it for you," and the Jester arose.

The Jester was out of the room in a flash
While the King wept morosely over his cash,
And the Queen and the Maid stood watching with fear
At each new enormous crocodile tear.

* By Pamela Prince Walker.

Then back came the Jester and there in his arms
Was a baby, all gurgling and gushing with charms,
So sweet was the innocent, delicate child
That when the King saw it he went quite wild.

"We'll give him a christening . . . we'll call him Joe!
And then we'll invite all the fairies we know!"
"I think," said the Queen, "that's as nice as can be,
But I don't think the baby's a 'he,' it's a 'she.' "

Well, the King thought a "she" would do nicely in school,
So cigars he did pass to the Maid and the Fool,
Then they all sat and listened, and soon from the dell
They heard the wee tinkle-tink-tink of a bell.

"The fairies are coming! What fun this will be!"
Cried the King as he galloped and giggled with glee.
Soon at the door there appeared a small Elf,
"The fairies!" he shouted, and jumped on a shelf.

Behold on the threshold a beautiful sight
All dressed in gossamer, silver and white,
A fairy danced in on the tips of her toes
And, curtsying, handed the baby a rose.

"This rose," she declared, "I want you to keep,
For it shall foretell of the bloom on your cheek."
And then in the doorway another appeared
In a cloak made of laces and organdy sheer.

"Keep this onyx of black, keep this jewel so rare,
For it shall foretell of your beauteous hair."
Now came the third, just as sweet as the rest,
She held in her hand a tiny bird's nest.

"This nest," she announced, "you must carefully mind,
It foretells of your soul, so gentle and kind."
Then into the room all the fairies did glide.
"Please give us a dance," the little Elf cried.

When the dancing was over the fairies did kneel,
"We christen her Beauty," they merrily pealed.
Then silently, silently back to their glade
The fairies tiptoed, and behind them the Maid.

And shortly the Jester did deign to retire,
And finally the Queen and the babe and her Sire.

SCENE 2

Many years passed and the baby grew fast
Until she was truly a beauteous lass.   *(Enter Beauty.)*
She sang from the time when she rose till she slept
And each of the presents she carefully kept.

Her youth and her voice gave the King so much joy
He forgot he had once hoped she would be a boy.
Only one in the land who did not love her well,
A horrible, hideous fairy called "Nell."   *(Enter Nell.)*

Now Nell was a terrible, frightening sight,
Her face it was green and her fingernails white,
Her hair was a color which no one had seen,
And she hated the King and she hated the Queen.

But most of all she hated our Beauty,
For at the christening she had not been included.
All day she spun cloth in a room in the tower,
And she plotted the death of the girl every hour.

One day the King and the Queen went away,
They left little Beauty and told her to play.
"Have fun," said the King, "I give you my trust,
But don't enter the tower, and that is a must."

The day went along and the Princess explored
Every room in the palace, each window, each door;
Evening came and the shadows did silently drop
As she came to the door of the tower and stopped.

"I shouldn't," she said to herself, "disobey,
But I've never been naughty before, so I may."
She opened the door and quietly crept
Up the stairs to the tower room, counting each step.

When she came to the top and turned the knob round
She heard from within a horrible sound,
"Come in, do come in," said a quavering voice,
Old Nell to herself did cruelly rejoice.

The door flew wide open and Beauty went in,
There sat Old Nell with a frightening grin,
"Come closer, my pretty one, closer," she cried,
And Beauty moved gracefully o'er to her side.

"My dear, I am tired, as tired as can be,
Would you sit here and spin just a little for me?"
"Why surely," said Beauty, and sat herself down,
"I'll spin till my family returns from the town."

No sooner had Beauty started to spin
Than she gave a small cry—she'd been pricked by a pin,
"Oh!" cried the child, and started to weep,
"I pricked myself, and now my eyes fill with sleep."

"Aha!" screamed the fairy, "I've had my revenge;
You'll sleep, my fair Beauty, for five years—for ten—
For the needle was touched with a poison so strong
You'll sleep on and on till a Prince comes along."

But before she had finished the child was asleep,
And out of the room the fairy did creep.
Then into the hall came the Queen and the King,
They soon fell asleep without saying a thing.

Behind them there entered the Fool and the Maid,
They soon fell to yawning and on the floor lay.
At last through the palace, so quiet and still,
There echoed Nell's laughter—oh, wicked and shrill.

SCENE 3

The years passed along, first four years, then eight,
And a creeping arbutus grew over the gate.
Another year passed and more vines grew high
Until they were nearly as tall as the sky.

The castle was covered by trees and by vines,
And through them the palace did show not a sign.
One day to this overgrown, foresty spot
A Prince came along with his horse at a trot.

He drew to a stop and stared at the trees,
"I wonder," he said, "What could lie behind these?"
He jumped off his horse and with one manly blow
He pushed through the shrubb'ry and stamped it below.

There was the palace all shining with light,
"My stars," said the Prince, "what a beautiful sight!"
He walked up the steps and pushed open the door,
When straight to his ears came a thunderous snore.

There on the floor lay the King and the Queen
And the Maid and the Jester, all sleeping serene.
The Prince threw his head back and laughed till he cried,
"This is so funny I think I shall die.

"Many things have I seen and will see many more,
But never a King sound asleep on the floor!"
He then stepped across them and looked all around
Till he came to the door of the tower in a bound.

Then up the long steps he did run till he got
To the room where the girl lay asleep on the cot.
"Why, this is the loveliest lass in the land!"
The Prince knelt beside her and lifted her hand.

Then slowly the Princess emitted a sigh,
And slowly, oh, slowly, she opened her eyes.

"My Prince," she murmured, "my Prince, you are here."
And she stood up and stretched, though she still felt
   quite queer.

And when she awakened, up sprang the King.
And the Queen, Maid, and Fool also did spring.
They yawned, and they stretched, and their eyes they
   did rub.
"What a nap!" growled the King. "Now where is the
   grub?"

The wedding was held that very same night,
And they say that the Princess looked lovely in white.
Then away did the couple trot on the steed,
While the family stood waving and calling "Godspeed."

So that is the story of our Sleeping Beauty,
And we certainly hope it has not been a duty
For you, but a pleasure,
To learn that they lived on quite happy forever!

How to Produce a Play

How to Produce a Play

BLOCKING AND CASTING THE PLAY

Blocking

After choosing a simple, imaginative, humorous play about which both she and the cast will be enthusiastic (see Introduction), the teacher is ready to block the action—that is, to plan the stage movement and position of characters at each moment in the play. It is a good idea to buy a notebook and draw a series of pictures depicting the exact changes in position of the characters, rather than blocking haphazardly during rehearsals.

Frequent Changes of Position

It is important that the blocking be exciting and full of variety. Frequent changes of position from standing to sitting, lying down to kneeling, make a more interesting spectacle than stationary stances. An entire scene played with two characters sitting upon a couch, for instance, would be very dull to watch; the audience might as well have stayed home and listened to it on the radio.

Use of Physical Activities

The teacher, now the director, may use a series of physical activities to keep the play alive and vibrant. Rather than leave the two characters sitting on the couch, she moves one of them to a table to arrange flowers or to dust, while the other ties his shoelace or leafs through a magazine. These activities must be carefully chosen to suit the character; Mama would dust the table, not Papa. They must also enhance the scene, not detract from it; in a moment of great excitement Mama would probably not dust the table at all, unless the director wanted to achieve a comic effect. In a "talky" scene the use of physical activities to hold the audience interest and keep the actors natural and relaxed is imperative. The director should be careful not to leave her characters standing or sitting with nothing to do for long periods of time.

Use of Exaggerated Positions

In a children's play comical or exaggerated positions may be used effectively. The director should avoid mundane blocking. It is more fun to see a character lie right down and roll over with laughter, than to see him stand still and chuckle. A haughty queen who enters with her nose in the air may trip over something and lose her dignity to the great amusement of the audience, whether this is written in the play or not. In an exciting moment the king may leap right up on the throne chair to make a proclamation, while the others scurry about, bump into each other, and fall down in the uproar. A timid character may jump at the slightest sound, or better yet, hide under a table or behind a chair. A bold character may stand with his legs wide apart and his hands on his hips. These actions need not be part of the written script. The director never should be afraid to move the characters up off the floor or down onto it in exaggerated positions. She must feel free to use colorful ideas of her own, and to use them as often as possible. These will give the play its "zing."

Sudden Changes for Effect

For effect, busy, exciting moments may be followed by sudden pauses ("stills"). Everyone is rushing about and talking at once—the trumpet blows offstage—sudden stillness—no one moves. After a pause, the first line is spoken in a whisper. These changes from loud to soft, from action to "still," keep the audience intrigued. A play must never run along on an even keel; it must have its ups and downs, its "fasts" and "slows," and it is up to the director to find these changes throughout the play and include them in the blocking.

Casting

Before she introduces the play to the children the teacher should cast it completely. This will avoid popularity contests in the classroom, which do little except cause hurt feelings. Besides, the children will readily agree that teacher knows best. There has been no tryout, for after the seven lessons she feels she knows the children's capabilities very well.

Much has been written and stated about casting a children's play. One school of thought on the subject holds that children's theater should be a kind of psychiatric clinic, in which children who "need help" are given long roles, whether they can handle them well or not, and in which shy children play bold character parts to develop their personalities, regardless of the effect upon the final production. Another one, somewhat more outdated, holds that "the play's the thing," not the children. This school worries about nothing except the actual performance and the audience reaction to it. The director from this school usually finds one or two extremely capable children and "stars" them in play after play.

The following solution to the casting problem adapts a little of each of the above schools of thought, omitting what seem to the author to be harmful consequences of both.

The Leading Roles

First, the director is careful to give the leading roles to competent children. Not only does it destroy the enthusiasm of the rest of the cast to have long stretches of the play bungled by an incompetent actor, but the child himself soon becomes aware of his own shortcomings (regardless of any amount of encouragement) and develops a growing feeling of inadequacy. If the child truly "needs help," this seems a poor way to help him. His brief moment of pleasure and success at being given the role will be far outweighed by his continuous failures during rehearsals and performance, and no amount of praise from the teacher can alter the obvious and painful truth. The same careful choice of actor is applied to the large character roles in the play.

A child with a reading or personality problem will be much happier with a small role which he can learn to handle successfully. Then perhaps his roles can slowly increase in importance along with his growing confidence in himself. After several ventures of playing small roles with increasing success he will be equipped for a larger part. In the meantime, there are many ways to make him feel an integral and important member of the group. (See Rehearsal Techniques.)

This is much the same principle which applies to the child who is afraid of water. Some teachers approve of taking him to the nearest diving board and throwing him in. It seems to the author a superior method is to let such a child play about in the shallow water for a while without making too much of an issue about his going deeper. Then, as he tries little by little to venture further, the teacher is careful to notice and praise him.

The Small Roles

Among the small roles in the play the director may take liberties with "type casting." Here she may encourage the shy boy to play the bold soldier, the defensive girl to play the sweet princess, and so on. If the part is only a few lines, this will not seriously impede the over-all production and will demand only a small extra amount of rehearsal time. In this way, taking a minor part of which he is capable and which stresses a quality in which he may be lacking, the child is benefited—and the production is unharmed.

Casting and Properties

Next, the director holds each child responsible for some set piece or property—to make it, bring it in, and see that it is on and off the stage at the correct times. The leading characters should be included in this, for they must be required to be just as helpful as the rest of the cast—no more, no less. It is not enough for them to contribute only their personalities to the play. Deciding which property each child will be responsible for when she casts the play, the director is ready to announce on the day she introduces the play the role each child will play and the property he must make.

Avoiding the Star System

Finally, when she does several productions with the same group, the director tries not to "star" the same children again and again. Most groups have enough versatility to avoid this, and after several plays some children who have played smaller roles may be ready to go one step farther into the deeper water.

Introducing the Play

After she has passed out the scripts the teacher announces she will read the play through once with the children following the lines in their scripts. Eager suggestions from the children that they be allowed to read should be refused. They will have plenty of opportunity to read in the future, and right now it will add much to their enthusiasm for the play to hear it read well and meaningfully.

When the reading is over and the children are quite delighted with the play, the teacher tells each one which role he will enact. This is a delicate business and must be handled carefully. It is obvious that the children playing the leading parts will be satisfied. For those with smaller roles, however, a few words from teacher may make the whole difference. Although the role is small, she points out, it is by far the funniest, scariest, or most beautiful part in the play. Each child must be made to feel he is a vital and fascinating part of the play—as truly he is, if the playwright has been writing especially for children's groups. Next, each child is encouraged to think of his character in terms of animal, leading center, or sphere. His imagination must be challenged, his feeling of importance in the group maintained, and this inspiration must start from the moment he receives his part.

At the end of the class period a little serious discussion of what is expected during rehearsals never hurts. It is expected that the children will arrive on time, and that they will quietly study their scripts offstage so that those onstage may concentrate easily. It is the teacher's business to think first of the group, and these are the limits she must impose for the benefit of the group as a whole. They are obviously just and fair ones. Repeated offenses upon these limits will surely result in disciplinary action, probably cause loss of the part altogether.

The discussion is ended with a note of optimism: "This is a beautiful play—very witty, very moving. I have seen you act in class and I know you can do a wonderful job with it, for each one of you has become an excellent actor. We'll have lots of fun putting it on. In fact, I can hardly wait to start rehearsing."

REHEARSAL TECHNIQUES

The "Bit" Players

After talking to several children's theater directors about their techniques during rehearsal, it would seem to the author that a common problem is that of occupying the children who are playing "bit" parts. These children, when they

are required to sit for long periods of time and watch the
others act, often constitute a serious discipline problem. Becoming bored with watching the repetition of one scene, and
feeling themselves more and more neglected, they are apt to
seek amusement by using various devices to draw the teacher's attention to themselves. Although this is annoying, it is,
after all, quite natural under the circumstances. Isn't it too
much to ask some children to sit quietly and twiddle their
thumbs while others receive all the attention and glory?

A Workable Solution

Happily, there are several answers to this difficulty. The
first one, and perhaps the best, is to make these "bit" players
feel of greater importance to the group by giving them a short
skit to rehearse. This skit, centered about the play itself, is
prepared to take about the city (into the schoolrooms, if possible, and onto the playgrounds) as an advertisement for the
play. The children, dressed in costume, enter, ringing a bell,
and make an announcement of the time and place of the
play, price of admission, and so on. This announcement may
be written in the form of a delightful poem, each child saying
one verse. The following is a typical such announcement for
a recent production of *Hansel and Gretel*. A little girl in
Dutch cap and costume entered, curtsied, and said:

"I am one little Dutch girl (tap, tap, tap),
 I am one little Dutch girl (clap, clap, clap),
 I am one little Dutch girl, that I be,
 And I got my cappy from a little Dutch tree."

A second girl then entered, curtsied, and together they said:

"We are two little Dutch girls (tap, tap, tap),
 We are two little Dutch girls (clap, clap, clap),
 We are two little Dutch girls, that we be,
 And we got our shoesies from a little Dutch tree."

When all the children had entered and repeated their verses, they announced the time and date of the play. This was followed by a short excerpt from the play, including the horrible Witch herself. Not only did the children have fun, but as a unique advertising scheme this could not have been surpassed. The largest audience we have ever had arrived for the production of *Hansel and Gretel*.

If a parent or older person is available to undertake its direction, rehearsals for the skit may take place in another room while regular rehearsals for the play are in progress. If no director can be found, the teacher herself may be required to designate special rehearsal days and prepare the skit herself. In either case, the bit players are not asked to come to rehearsals for the regular play while they prepare their advertising stunt. Preparation for the stunt may be arranged to last for very nearly the duration of the rehearsal schedule for the play. By the time they have given their stunt these children need only attend the last few run-throughs to learn their parts in the major productions.

When it is necessary to ask these bit players to rehearse with the rest of the cast before the last few run-throughs, it should be arranged that they do so only for the few minutes it takes for their special parts. Then they should be excused to return to work on their own small performance.

The Bit Players and the Final Run-throughs

During the final run-throughs and dress rehearsal, when the entire cast must be present, the teacher should find special duties for the actors playing small roles. One child may take notes of her suggestions as the director watches the scene (so the actors need not be interrupted). One may sit in the back of the room and jot down the moments when he finds it is difficult to hear. One may pull the curtains and prompt. Several may paint large, bright pictures of the characters in the play; these will be cut out and pasted upon posters to advertise the play. Several may paint small pictures pertaining to the story on each program. Several may decorate the entrance to the theater, or the ticket booth, with gay crepe paper streamers. At all times the small helpers must keep an ear cocked for their own entrance cues. Thus, the problem of disciplining children who are sitting about the theater with nothing to do has been solved by refusing to allow the situation to arise to begin with.

Dual Casting

It is well to mention here the solution of dual casting—that is, producing the play for two nights in succession with different casts, so that each child may play a large role. If two directors may be found, or if the teacher has time to prepare both plays (for exactly twice as many rehearsals will be required), this may be done successfully. However, the advertising stunt seems a more workable idea, both from the point of view of time and because the children chosen for small parts are usually not qualified to tackle the leading roles.

Taking the Play Slowly

In planning her rehearsal schedule the teacher should allow two full rehearsals of each scene for the blocking alone. After this, two full rehearsals should be devoted to each scene with the lines learned. Two more rehearsals of each act should be included before she begins a single run-through. Except for the preliminary readings, the play should be rehearsed in small pieces first and put together later. She will find this gives her plenty of time to work out each small moment effectively. It is most difficult, if not impossible, to rehearse the whole play from beginning to end during each rehearsal.

The Call Board

A call board, or bulletin board, may be erected at the theater entrance with the rehearsal schedule carefully listed upon it, along with the dates when the lines must be learned. The children may copy this schedule in their scripts and refer to it when they wish, rather than bothering the director with their questions.

A FEW HINTS FOR SUCCESSFUL TEACHING

In only one instance have I found it necessary to remove a child from his role in a play. This was done after every means of praise, encouragement, and quiet reminders of the limits which must exist during rehearsal period had been exhausted. A final warning was given, which went unheeded, and the child was replaced, much to the relief of the others in the class—and much to my sorrow.

In general, however, the following suggestions to the teacher will enhance workable, if not perfect, relationships in the creative classroom.

Praise

Surprisingly many teachers choose criticism as their means of imparting knowledge. They look carefully for the mistakes the children make, and are certain to mention them. They smile only upon occasion (usually through their teeth). They teach by fear.

The teacher who chooses praise for her medium of imparting knowledge watches carefully for the "good" things that happen in class, and never fails to mention them. She softpedals many of the mistakes. The more difficult the child, the more responsibility she feels to notice his first helpful action and to praise it—not with superlatives, out of all proportion to his small gesture, but with a few quiet words—"Good,

Johnny boy, very good indeed!" She teaches by love. In short, she is a teacher, not a drama critic.

It is not hard for us to realize the importance of praise when we look into our own lives, and our own hearts, for the pride and renewed vigor we find there after a few complimentary words, sincerely spoken.

Questions, then Action

Children are noted for their brief span of concentration. It is hard for them to sit still and listen for long periods of time. The teacher who makes explanations as brief as possible, and who breaks them up with questions, is a wise one.

Imagine a child who is using a hearing aid. When he is bored with the talk around him he can click off his aid and sit happily with his own, far more interesting thoughts. However, if he knows there is the possibility of a question being asked him at any moment, he must keep his aid tuned high and listen carefully in order to answer it. All children have imaginary hearing aids which they may tune on or off at will. In a long-winded explanation the teacher can see the hearing aids being clicked off one by one. As soon as she asks a question, however, the class clicks to attention, little ears grow two sizes bigger, and she has succeeded in gaining interest.

After a brief explanation and discussion period, enhanced by questions, the wise teacher moves quickly to the exercise. "Out of your seats. Let's see you do it." No matter if everyone does not yet understand the principle. The exercise will help, and at the end of the class period another brief questioning will bring along the stragglers. By acting, not by talking, do children learn to act.

Enthusiasm

Nothing can inspire a class more quickly than an enthusiastic teacher. Nothing can make them more happy than a hearty laugh or a burst of spontaneous applause from her. Luckily, children's dramatics is a subject which includes many points to arouse her enthusiasm. The exercises can vary into infinity if the teacher will take time to create new ones; even the same exercise can look entirely different as it is acted by two different groups. There are many highly imaginative children's plays on the market with humor and originality that adult plays seldom encompass. If the teacher really enjoys children, their easygoing, spontaneous creations will always be fun to watch.

Only two things can seriously damage this enthusiasm. A perfectionist attitude, first adopted by the teacher, then instilled into the children, is the first one. Each line must be spoken with just this inflection; each gesture is copied carefully from teacher and repeated again and again. Result: a perfect play without a spark of life in it given by a disenchanted cast.

The other attitude which destroys enthusiasm is the overly casual one. Here the teacher has set no standard of performance—or rather of responsibility. Many of the children have never really learned their lines. No suggestions have been made in rehearsal to "spice the play up" a bit. No appeal has been made to the children to add their own original touches to their business or characterizations. They have not been held responsible to make their own set pieces or bring their own props. Result: one of those plays about which parents say, "Never mind—children are always cute to watch anyway!"

There is a happy medium between these two opposite attitudes. Hold the children completely responsible for their lines, props, and sets—then relax, encourage and enjoy. Mostly enjoy. After all, acting is supposed to be fun!

Three Plays

PRODUCTION INFORMATION

Land of Jesters
Royalty—none; Running time—30 minutes; Rehearsal time —12 hour-long rehearsals; Age group of actors—5th through 8th grades; Age group of audience—2nd through 8th grades.

Rumpelstiltskin
Royalty—$10; Running time—45 minutes; Rehearsal time —16 hour-long rehearsals; Age group of actors—5th through 8th grades; Age group of audience—2nd through 8th grades.

Around the World in Eighty Days
Royalty—$15; Running time—1½ hours; Rehearsal time— 25 hour-long rehearsals; Age group of actors—7th through 9th grades; Age group of audience—4th through 9th grades.

NOTE: The parts of Passepartout, Fogg, and Fix, being long and rather difficult, may be played by exceptional 8th or 9th grade boys, or if possible, by high school students. Additional information for producing is given in the play.

For permission to use these plays, write Hill and Wang, Inc., 104 Fifth Avenue, New York 11, N. Y.

Land of Jesters

by

PAMELA PRINCE WALKER

Characters (*in order of appearance*)

JAIL GUARD
LAWYER
BUTCHER
BAKER
CANDLESTICK MAKER
ELF
TWO JESTERS
QUEEN SNOOTY
PRINCESS LOVELY
FOUR PRINCESSES

The scene is Main Street of the Land of Jesters. On one side of the stage is a sign saying "Land of Jesters"; on the other a sign saying "Main Street." At stage right are three small tables decked with gay tablecloths. One bears a sign saying "Butcher," one "Baker," and the third "Candlestick Maker." Center-stage is a sign saying "Lawyer's Office." Under it are a stool and small desk with books on it. Next to the Lawyer's office is a brightly decorated stool for the Queen. At far left is a circle on the floor and next to it a sign saying "Jail." A bench stands next to the circle on which the GUARD is found sound asleep. The LAWYER sits in his office reading a book. The BUTCHER, BAKER, and CANDLESTICK MAKER

stand behind their respective tables holding a still position—
the BUTCHER sharpening his knives, the BAKER holding a tray
of goodies, the CANDLESTICK MAKER with his candle.

Enter from right a little elf riding a bicycle with schoolbooks in the basket. He stops at the sign saying "Land of
Jesters" and reads it aloud, scratching his head. Then he
parks his bicycle and moves across the stage, looking at each
character with interest. The characters hold their positions
very still, however, and do not raise their eyes as he passes.

ELF (*scratching his head as he comes down center to the
audience*): It says "Land of Jesters" (*pointing to the sign*) but
I don't see a jester anywhere. There's a butcher and a baker
and a candlestick maker—also a lawyer and a jail-keeper—
but no jester at all. So why call it "Land of Jesters"? (*He sits
on the floor.*) Whew, I'm tired. I've come a long way on my
bicycle—all the way from the United States of America, and
believe me, that's a lo-o-o-ong way. (*Lying back and propping
his chin on his elbow.*) Would you like to know why I came?
All right, I'll tell you. It's because where I come from I go
to school. Everyone my age has to go to school in the United
States of America—even if they're elves like me. It's not that
I mind going to school so much, and the children are very
nice to me there. But here's the rub! (*He jumps up, turns
his back to the audience, and waves his tail.*) My tail! No one
has a tail in the United States of America—not even the elves
—and everyone laughs and laughs at me. It's very embarrass-
ing. I tried to pull it off, but it won't come—see? (*He tugs
his tail.*) So I thought I'd go for a ride on my bicycle and find
a place where people had tails—like me. Then I'd stay there
forever and never go home again. An elf without a country!
(*Wailing.*) But the people here don't have tails either. It's
very sad! (*He sits on the floor and cries softly.*)

(*Gradually the people behind him come to life. First they*

*look at him curiously. Then they run to the bicycle and be-
gin to talk in excited whispers. Apparently they have never
seen a bicycle before. They take the books from the basket
and begin to examine them. The* ELF *suddenly realizes what's
going on, and stands up quickly.)*

ELF: Hey! What are you doing?

*(The people rush back to their places, taking the books
with them. The* ELF *hurries to the* BUTCHER, *who stands with
the* BAKER *and* CANDLESTICK MAKER, *reading an arithmetic
book.)*

ELF: Hey, give me back my arithmetic book. I haven't
done my homework yet.

BUTCHER: My dear boy, this is very interesting. Very interesting indeed!

BAKER *(reading)*: "Two plus two equals four." *(They all
laugh.)*

CANDLESTICK MAKER: Ho, ho! How funny! Everyone
knows two plus two equals five.

BUTCHER and BAKER: Of course!

ELF: It does not. In the United States, where I come from,
two plus two equals four.

BUTCHER: But here in the Land of Jesters two plus two
equals five.

BAKER and CANDLESTICK MAKER: Of course!

ELF: Well, never mind. I guess in different places things
are different. Tell me, please—*(he grabs their hands)* since
things are different here, do any of the people wear tails?

BUTCHER *(puzzled)*: Tails?

ELF *(tugging his tail)*: Yes, tails—like this.

(The BUTCHER, BAKER, *and* CANDLESTICK MAKER *all turn
around and look at their behinds. Then they shake their
heads.)*

BUTCHER: No! No tails!

ELF *(sadly)*: Phooey!

CANDLESTICK MAKER (*laughing*): Look at this. (*He points to the arithmetic book.*) This is better yet. One plus one equals two. (*They all dissolve in laughter.*)

ELF: Please give me back my book. If no one here wears a tail, I might as well go back home and do my lessons.

BUTCHER: My dear boy, please don't go yet. This book is the funniest thing I've seen in ages.

ELF: In the United States no one thinks it's funny at all. Besides, if no one has a tail—

BAKER (*angrily*): Why do you keep harping on the subject of tails?

CANDLESTICK MAKER: That's what I say! What difference does it make whether we have tails or not?

BUTCHER: Yes, I'm tired of hearing about tails. Leave us alone and let us read your arithmetic book. (*They go back to reading the book.*)

ELF: Now you give me that book. That's my book, and you had no business stealing it in the first place. If no one here wears a tail I am certainly going back to the United States where at least the people know that two plus two equals four.

BUTCHER, BAKER, CANDLESTICK MAKER: Two plus two equals five.

ELF: Four!

BUTCHER, BAKER, CANDLESTICK MAKER: Five!

ELF (*grabbing his book and running down the street*): Four, four, four!

(*The* BUTCHER, BAKER, *and* CANDLESTICK MAKER *dash after him. Round and round they go. The* LAWYER *comes out of his office. The* JAIL GUARD *looks up from the comic book he has chosen from the bicycle basket.*)

LAWYER: Say, say, what goes on here? (*He catches the* ELF *by the ear. The others stop running.*)

ELF: I'm sorry, sir, but they stole my book.

LAWYER (*shaking his finger at the pursuers*): Shame! You shouldn't have done that. Now go back to your shops. (*They hang their heads and return to the tables.*) Won't you come into my office and maybe we can straighten this out.

ELF: No, I'd better go home, since no one here has a tail.

LAWYER: A tail?

ELF: Yes. (*He tugs at his tail dejectedly.*)

LAWYER: Oh, I see. Well, you come in and let's talk this over. Perhaps I can help you.

ELF (*walking around the LAWYER and looking carefully at his back*): No, it's no use. (*He starts to go.*)

LAWYER (*catching the ELF by the arm*): Come, boy. I'm the best lawyer in the Land of Jesters—even if I haven't a tail. I can solve all kinds of difficult problems.

ELF: Well—

LAWYER: Come ahead, now. (*They enter the office and sit, the* LAWYER *on the stool, the* ELF *perched sadly on the desk.*) Now, you want to find a place where people have tails. (*The* ELF *shakes his head in assent.*) Because people laugh at yours. (*The* ELF *shakes his head.*) And they laugh because it's different. (*The* ELF *shakes his head.*) Why, my dear boy, it's a *blessing* to be different. Nowadays everyone tries to be the same as everyone else. It makes them so—so dull. It's much better to have big ears, or a big nose—or even a tail. Then you really *are* someone.

ELF: Who?

LAWYER: Why, *yourself,* of course. And nobody else.

ELF: Well, I don't want to be myself, if it has to have a tail.

LAWYER: Then, my boy, I'm afraid you've come to the wrong place. (*Shaking his head darkly.*) The wrong place, indeed. This is the Land of Jesters, so called because it has a Queen who makes everyone laugh at each other, whether they want to or not. (*He takes a book of American history from underneath him.*)

ELF: My American history book!

LAWYER: I didn't steal it, mind you. I just—borrowed it. I've been reading your Constitution. It's a very friendly one. Perhaps you should go back to the United States. Our Constitution isn't nearly so friendly. (*He hands the book back to the* ELF.)

ELF (*sighing*): Well, thank you anyway.

LAWYER: Oh, that's all right. I'm afraid I haven't done much good. I can see you still aren't proud of just being yourself.

ELF: Not as long as I have this ugly old thing tagging along behind me.

LAWYER: I realize it's hard to be laughed at. If people knew how hard it was I don't think they'd do so much of it. But you'll have to leave here immediately, or you'll really be in trouble. You see, here we only have one law in our Constitution—only one. (*He takes up a piece of paper saying "Constitution—Land of Jesters" and reads.*) "The Queen of the Land of Jesters hereby states that when she laughs at a joke, everyone in the land must also laugh. He or she who does not laugh when the Queen does will be thrown into the jailhouse to await execution. Signed: Queen Snooty, Queen of the Land of Jesters. P.S.—Whether he wants to or not."

ELF: Whether who wants to what?

LAWYER: To laugh.

ELF: Oh!

LAWYER: So you see you had better run quickly before Queen Snooty comes. The first thing she will do will be laugh at your tail, and then everyone will be obliged to laugh at it—even though they really don't want to at all.

ELF: Horrors! (*He rushes to the door.*) Thank you for

everything. I'm on my way home where we have a friendly Constitution and where two plus two equals four.

BUTCHER, BAKER, CANDLESTICK MAKER: Two plus two equals five.

ELF (*hesitating*): Oh, never mind, I haven't time for that now. (*He rushes to the bicycle and starts to put the books in the basket. The sound of trumpets in the distance.*)

LAWYER (*calling from the door of his office*): Hurry, here she comes. (*To the others.*) He's unhappy when people laugh at his tail.

BUTCHER: So that's why he had that phobia about tails.

BAKER: I understand now.

CANDLESTICK MAKER: We're sorry we weren't nicer.

BUTCHER, BAKER, CANDLESTICK MAKER: And we're sorry we stole your books.

LAWYER: Don't bother him now. He's in a hurry.

BUTCHER, BAKER, CANDLESTICK MAKER: Yes, hurry, hurry. (*The sound of trumpets comes nearer. The ELF is on his bicycle and starting to ride away.*)

GUARD (*standing*): Hey you. Here's your comic book. (*He waves it in the air.*) Come back, come back. Here's your comic book. (*The ELF starts back for his book. A blast of trumpets. Two little JESTERS appear.*)

JESTERS: Make way for the Queen! (*All the people fall to the floor, as the QUEEN enters, flanked by five PRINCESSES. Four of them stand behind her. One wanders down and sits on the bench next to the jail.*)

QUEEN (*sitting on the stool haughtily*): Princess Lovely, don't you want to sit here with your sisters?

PRINCESS LOVELY: No, thank you, Mother.

4 PRINCESSES (*haughtily*): She's too good for us!

PRINCESS LOVELY (*sweetly*): That isn't it at all. I just like this bench, if you don't mind, Mother.

QUEEN: Very well, miss, stay where you are. But you'd

better be careful. You are becoming very, very democratic lately. I don't like it at all.

PRINCESS LOVELY: Yes, Mother.

QUEEN: And I have noticed it becomes more and more difficult for you to laugh when I do. You know the Constitution. When the Queen laughs, so laughs the world—even the Princesses.

4 PRINCESSES: We always do.

PRINCESS LOVELY: It's only because you laugh at other people instead of with them. It seems so cruel. Couldn't you try to laugh just when things are truly funny?

QUEEN: You be careful, miss. I warn you.

PRINCESS LOVELY: And, Mother, you never, never laugh at yourself. (*The people applaud.*)

QUEEN (*jumping up*): Be quiet. Quiet—all of you. I've had enough. (*Silence.*) We are gathered here to laugh, and laugh we will. Who has the first joke today?

BUTCHER (*shakily*): I have, Your Majesty.

QUEEN: Repeat it!

BUTCHER (*coming center, his legs shaking*): What's black and white and red all over?

QUEEN (*leaning forward*): I don't know. What?

BUTCHER (*in terror*): A newspaper. (*Silence.*)

QUEEN: That's not funny. (*The* BUTCHER *falls back on his knees.*)

BAKER: I have one, Your Majesty.

QUEEN (*sighing*): Repeat it!

BAKER (*center*):

> I never saw a Purple Cow,
> I never hope to see one;
> But I can tell you, anyhow,
> I'd rather see than be one.

(PRINCESS LOVELY *laughs and claps.*)

QUEEN: Silence! That's not funny either. It's not even a joke—it's a poem.

PRINCESS LOVELY: It's cute, though.

QUEEN: Well, who wouldn't rather see a purple cow than be one? For myself I can think of nothing worse than being a purple cow. It makes me shudder to think of it. (*The* BAKER *retires.*)

CANDLESTICK MAKER (*venturing forward shyly*): I just saw something funny in an arithmetic book, Your Majesty. It came from the United States and it said—two plus two equals four. (*Everyone laughs except the* QUEEN.)

QUEEN: Silence! That isn't funny, it's peculiar. Where did you get this arithmetic book, Candlestick Maker?

CANDLESTICK MAKER: From him! (*He points to the* ELF. *Immediately he realizes his mistake, as everyone gasps in horror.*)

QUEEN: What? Who is this?

4 PRINCESSES: Yes, who is this?

EVERYONE: Yes, who is this?

ELF (*standing*): I am an elf, Your Majesty—from the United States of America.

QUEEN: Come forward. (*The* ELF *steps forward.*) I didn't know there were elves in the United States of America.

ELF: Oh yes indeed, Your Majesty. There are quite a few of us. But most of us don't have tails any more.

(*The people wave at him desperately, trying to get him to be quiet.*)

QUEEN: Tails?

ELF (*not seeing the people*): Like this, Your Majesty. (*He pulls his tail. The* QUEEN *looks at it for a long moment. Then she leans back on the stool and laughs. She laughs and laughs.*)

QUEEN (*wiping her eyes*): Laugh, everyone. Laugh! (*The people laugh weakly.*) Louder, louder! (*They laugh louder. The* ELF *sits on the ground dejectedly. His lip trembles.*)

Laugh, Lawyer. Harder! Laugh, daughters! (*The four* PRIN-
CESSES *laugh in high, staccato giggles.*)

PRINCESS LOVELY (*rushing to the* ELF, *putting her arms
around him*): Be quiet, all of you! (*Silence falls.*)

QUEEN: What is the meaning of this?

PRINCESS LOVELY: Stop them, Mother. Can't you see you're
hurting his feelings dreadfully?

QUEEN: Princess Lovely, return to your bench immediately.

PRINCESS LOVELY: I won't. It's time something was done
about this. It isn't right for you to abuse your power so.

ELF: At least we don't have cruel queens in the United
States of America.

QUEEN: Lovely, return to your room at the palace. You
shall have bread and milk for supper. The Constitution com-
mands—

LAWYER (*shouting*): Amend the Constitution!

ELF: They do it at home.

EVERYONE: Yes, amend, amend!

QUEEN: Rabble-rouser! Guard, take that man. Clap him
in jail. (*The* GUARD *advances to the* LAWYER.)

PRINCESS LOVELY: If he goes, Mother, I go too.

QUEEN (*smiling*): It's your own choice, my dear. Guard,
take the Princess as well.

(*The guard takes the* PRINCESS *and* LAWYER *to the jail.
They step calmly inside the circle. The* PRINCESS *rests her
head upon the* LAWYER's *shoulder.*)

QUEEN (*still smiling*): Anyone else? (*Silence.*) Very well,
we will proceed to the execution in a moment.

4 PRINCESSES: An execution! What fun! (*They giggle.*)

QUEEN (*yawning*): But first, the royal nap. Excitement always makes me so sleepy, and I must be wide-awake for the
great event.

4 PRINCESSES: Aw, let's do it now, Mother.

QUEEN: In a little while, my darlings. First the nap.

4 PRINCESSES (*sadly*): Oh, golly.

QUEEN (*sleepily*): Hush now, hush. We must all take a little nap. It is the Queen's desire, and my babies will always obey the Queen's desire, won't they?

4 PRINCESSES (*sadly*): Yes, Mother.

(*The* QUEEN *kneels on the ground, her head in her arms, her behind in the air.*)

QUEEN (*sleepily*): Come everyone—to sleep. (*Everyone kneels in like position, except the prisoners.*) To sleep. (*There is a loud snore from all.*)

ELF (*rising anxiously, hurrying to the jail—in a whisper*): Can't you just run away? There aren't any doors on this jail.

PRINCESS LOVELY: No, little elf. You see this circle on the floor. It is magic, and we cannot cross it.

LAWYER (*sadly*): The only way we can escape is for the guard to use his magic key.

ELF: You mean—this one, hanging from his belt? (*The* PRINCESS *and* LAWYER *nod sadly.*) Shh. I will steal it from him, and let you out.

PRINCESS: You mustn't. It's wrong to steal.

ELF: He stole my comic book, didn't he?

PRINCESS: Yes, but—

LAWYER: According to the laws anywhere, one theft does not justify another, however—

ELF: Oh, phooey! You two are just too good for your own breeches (*he bows to the* PRINCESS)—and petticoats. (*Turning to the audience.*) Don't you think I should steal the key and help them escape? —Good, I will then. You two look the other way if it bothers you so much. (*The Princess and the* LAWYER *turn their heads, as the* ELF *reaches for the key.*)

GUARD (*opening an eye*): You'd better watch it!

ELF: It's no use. He's awake. Oh, dear, what shall we do? (*Slowly.*) Wait! I have an idea! If someone in the audience just has a safety pin—does anyone have a safety pin he can lend me? (*A child in the front row hands the* ELF *a safety pin.*) And scissors. Does anyone have a pair of scissors? (*Someone hands him a pair of scissors.*) I will just cut off part of my tail (*he does so*). That doesn't hurt at all. I've tried cutting it off completely, but it just grows back in again. And now, I will pin it on the Queen—so! (*The* PRINCESS *and* LAWYER *gasp.*) Now, when she awakens—oh, oh! First, you must tell me, has the Queen ever seen a safety pin?

LAWYER: I doubt it. We never use them here.

ELF: I didn't think so. How could people who think two plus two equals five ever make sensible things like safety pins! Now, when she awakens—

(*The* QUEEN *stirs.*)

ELF: Shh.

QUEEN (*standing and stretching*): Mmm, what a nice nap! Now we are ready for the execution. (*She runs about, kicking everyone.*) Wake up. Wake up, everyone. (*Everyone stands.*) We are ready for the executions.

4 PRINCESSES: Oh, goody!

QUEEN (*sitting on the throne*): Guard, open the jail-house. (*The* GUARD *opens the jail with his magic key.*) Jesters, escort the Princess and the Lawyer to the center of the street. (*They do so.*) Are your arrows ready?

JESTERS: Yes, Your Majesty!

Queen: Good. Prepare to shoot. (*The* JESTERS *stand back and prepare to shoot their arrows—which have red hearts on the tips.*) When they shoot now, everyone must laugh. (*The four* PRINCESSES *giggle.*) Not yet! I said when they shoot. (*The* PRINCESSES *stop.*) Ready, set—

ELF: One moment, Your Majesty!

QUEEN: What is it?

ELF: I must whisper something of very great importance to Your Majesty first.

QUEEN: Well, hurry, hurry. We are ready to begin. (ELF *whispers excitedly in* QUEEN's *ear.*) What? What are you saying?

ELF: It's true, Your Majesty. It must have grown there while you were sleeping.

QUEEN: I don't believe it!

ELF: Well, look for yourself.

(*The* QUEEN *jumps from the stool, turns her back to the audience, and tries to peek over her shoulder at her tail. Everyone on stage shouts with laughter.*)

QUEEN (*tugging it*): Take it off. Take this ugly thing off me immediately. You put it there—you must have.

ELF: I did, Your Majesty, and I will—just as soon as you release the prisoners.

QUEEN (*shrieking*): Release the prisoners!

(*The* JESTERS *put down their bows. The* PRINCESS *and the* LAWYER *hug each other happily.*)

ELF: And amend the Constitution.

QUEEN: Amend the Constitution then. Anything! I don't care. (*A great shout from all the people.*) But take this off me, you—you—you democratic elf. Take it off me, do you hear? (*She chases the* ELF *across the stage, as the people howl with laughter.*)

ELF (*while running*): Please, Your Majesty, how can I remove the tail while you're running after me?

QUEEN (*stamping her foot*): Here, then! (*She stands still. The* ELF *removes the tail and holds it up for all to see.*)

PRINCESS LOVELY: What a lovely little tail. It saved our lives. It amended our Constitution. Please, little elf, would you pin it on me? I should like to wear it forever.

ELF: This—ugly tail?

PRINCESS LOVELY: It's not ugly. Don't you ever say so again. It's a beautiful tail.

ELF (*blushing*): Very well, my lady. If you really wish it.

PRINCESS: I do. (*The* ELF *pins the tail on the* PRINCESS.)

QUEEN: Hmpf! People who think purple cows are cute, and tails are beautiful!

PRINCESS LOVELY: Are better than people who never dare to be different, and who laugh at those who do.

LAWYER: That's a wonderful moral for our story, Princess Lovely.

ELF: I will never be afraid to be different again.

PRINCESS LOVELY: I think it would be nice if we all closed our eyes really tight, and said, as if we really meant it (*she does so*)—"I will never be afraid to be different again."

EVERYONE (*with eyes tight shut*): I will never be afraid to be different again.

ELF: And now, I must go home and do my homework.

GUARD: Here's your comic book.

ELF (*taking the book and climbing on his bicycle*): Thank you, guard. Good-by, everyone. (*He throws a kiss to the* PRINCESS.) Good-by, Princess Lovely.

PRINCESS LOVELY: Come back to visit us.

ELF: I will. (*He starts off.*)

BUTCHER, BAKER, CANDLESTICK MAKER: But two plus two do equal five!

ELF (*as he goes into the distance*): That's right. Be different. But four is the correct answer, really.

BUTCHER, BAKER, CANDLESTICK MAKER: Five!

ELF (*in distance*): Four.

BUTCHER, BAKER, CANDLESTICK MAKER: Five!

ELF (*way away now*): Four.

BUTCHER, BAKER, CANDLESTICK MAKER (*after debating quickly with each other*): All right, four then. Good-by!

(*They stand waving, as the curtain falls.*)

Rumpelstiltskin

Adaptation, including poetry, by

PAMELA PRINCE WALKER

Characters (*in order of appearance*)

> TOWNSPEOPLE
> HO-HUM, THE PALACE GUARD
> FLOWER GIRL
> NEWCOMER
> SILK MERCHANT
> MILLER
> MARY ANN, HIS DAUGHTER
> JESTER
> MAIDIE
> KING
> QUEEN
> PRINCE
> RUMPELSTILTSKIN

ACT 1

SCENE 1

The village market place at noon. There is much activity. A group of young girls surround a wagonload of flowers; several old ladies bicker energetically around a vegetable cart;

a silk merchant runs about trying to sell his wares. On one side of the stage stand the palace gates. A young man leans against them, chewing an apple. As the curtains open, he saunters forward. Stopping center-stage, he surveys the audience, and clears his throat—loudly. The people on stage turn to watch him.

Ho-Hum (*to the audience*): Welcome! (*He looks about him, clears his throat again, and speaks in a louder voice.*) Welcome, everyone! (*Again he pauses. The people on stage applaud enthusiastically.*) My name is Ho-Hum. I am, so to speak, the master of ceremonies for our play. But in real life I am a guard at the palace. That is why I was leaning against the palace gates chewing an apple. Or perhaps I should say, that is why I was leaning against the palace gates. I was chewing an apple because I like apples! (*He pauses, and once more everyone on stage applauds.*) Besides, you might as well chew an apple if you're guarding a palace. After all, these days nothing much of any importance happens to palaces.

Flower Girl: Except Rumpelstiltskin!

Ho-Hum: Oh yes, Rumpelstiltskin! That's what I wanted to tell you about. You see, that's the only really important thing that ever happened to us. Now, my name is Ho-Hum, and I am the palace guard! (*He looks around importantly.*)

Flower Girl: On with the play!

Ho-Hum: And that is the flower girl! She is of no importance to the plot whatsoever! (*The* Flower Girl *curtsies prettily.*) That man with the eager look is the newcomer. (*The* Newcomer *executes a graceful bow.*) And the rest are —people in the cast. (*Everyone bows.*)

Ho-Hum (*behind his hand to the audience*): They aren't important either, but they think they are, so if you would applaud, it would make them very happy.

(*The audience applauds with* Ho-Hum.)

EVERYONE ON STAGE: On with the play!

HO-HUM: Oh, yes! On with the play!

(HO-HUM *takes his place by the palace gates, the people turn back to their activities, and the play begins.*)

SILK MERCHANT (*running to the* NEWCOMER): Silks and shoelaces! Silks and shoelaces!

NEWCOMER: I see the silks, but where are the laces?

SILK MERCHANT (*offended*): Very well, if you don't want to buy anything you don't have to. (*Moving off.*) Silks and shoelaces! Silks and shoelaces!

NEWCOMER (*scratching his head*): What a quaint place! First a palace guard makes a speech which is utterly unintellegible, and then a man tries to sell me shoelaces when he doesn't have any to sell. (*Sitting down.*) It makes me quite tired! I do hope nothing else happens today!

(*From off stage comes a loud cry. Everyone peers off.*)

FLOWER GIRL (*casually*): It's only the miller whipping his daughter again.

EVERYONE: Oh, is that all!

SILK MERCHANT: They say he's trying to teach her how to spin straw into gold.

A WOMAN: Well, when it comes to spinning, he's an expert. No one has ever spun a tale as well as he.

(*Another loud cry from off stage.* HO-HUM *yawns noisily.*)

NEWCOMER (*jumping to his feet*): How can you stand there and listen to that? Why don't you do something about it?

SILK MERCHANT (*behind his hand to the* FLOWER GIRL): Another rabble-rouser.

FLOWER GIRL (*nodding*): We get them every so often.

SILK MERCHANT (*politely*): That's a fine idea, young man! What would you suggest?

NEWCOMER: Take the miller to court on a charge of daughter-beating.

SILK MERCHANT: We have a king in there (*pointing to the*

palace) who is very fond of beheading people. If you asked him politely, he might oblige.

FLOWER GIRL: Either with the miller's head for spanking his daughter, or with yours for telling him about it.

(*There is another loud cry from off stage.*)

NEWCOMER: Ho-Hum, you run and get the miller. Bring him here. I'll tell him a thing or two about whipping children, if all of you are afraid to.

HO-HUM (*dislodging himself from his comfortable position against the gates*): If you'll just see to it that no one invades the palace while I'm gone—

NEWCOMER (*leaning against the gates*): I'd be glad to.

HO-HUM: Would you like to chew my apple till I get back?

NEWCOMER: No thank you!

(HO-HUM *exits. Everyone watches the* NEWCOMER.)

MILLER (*off stage*): Crying? There's been no crying here. You heard the wind sighing through the trees.

HO-HUM (*off stage*): It was not the wind.

MILLER: The loud *whir* of our spinning wheel?

HO-HUM (*with a yawn*): Come with me, or we shall have to behead you. *Hup,* two, three, four. *Hup,* two, three, four. (HO-HUM, *the* MILLER, *and the* MILLER's *daughter march on stage.*) Halt, one, two. Right face!

(*The* MILLER *and his daughter,* MARY ANN, *stand before the* NEWCOMER. *The* MILLER *leans on his cane;* MARY ANN, *a pretty girl, weeps into a large handkerchief and occasionally blows her nose.*)

NEWCOMER: So this is the miller who beats his daughter?

MILLER: So this is the newcomer I have heard so much about? What a handsome chap!

NEWCOMER (*pleased, in spite of himself*): Come, come!

MILLER: You have a most beautiful face, sir. If I knew how to paint, I would paint it. Would you like a gumdrop?

NEWCOMER (*reaching for the bag*): My dear sir, how did you know? I *adore* gumdrops. (*At this point,* MARY ANN *emits a dreadful wail.*) But, gumdrops or no, we must get on with the business.

MILLER (*obligingly*): By all means! (*Poking* MARY ANN *in the ribs.*) Curtsy, and say "How do you do."

MARY ANN (*curtsying*): How do you do. (*She hiccups.*)

NEWCOMER: How do you do.

MILLER (*poking her again*): Now, tell him why you're crying.

MARY ANN: I am crying because— (*She hiccups.*)

MILLER (*quickly*): She is crying because she is so happy!

(*They all look at him, dumbfounded. Suddenly, the* FLOWER GIRL *laughs.*)

FLOWER GIRL: Very well, old man. Let's hear your latest story.

(*Everyone laughs, and there are calls of "Story!" The* MILLER *moves to the center of the group, and raises his hand. A silence falls. Even* MARY ANN *forgets to cry, and stands, wide-eyed, waiting for him to begin.*)

MILLER: Once upon a time there was a miller who lived with his daughter in a small house. This miller was old and very poor, but his daughter was young and very talented. (MARY ANN *hiccups.*) Every day these two would rise early and go to work, she to her spinning, and he to his plans and schemes for the future. Every night they would fall into bed, and await the next day's drudgery. One day the miller and his daughter arose as usual and went to work, never dreaming that this day was to be fateful. Indeed, this day was to mark a bright new era—not only for the hapless two, but also for their town and country! (*The people move forward, murmuring "Go on" and "Continue."*) The daughter sat beside her spinning wheel, sighed a little, raised her hand, and touched the wheel. Lo! Upon the floor dropped a tiny piece of gold!

(*A chuckle and murmur from the crowd.*) Amazed, she reached forward again, and this time a shower of gold fell before her. Each time she touched the wheel more gold poured forth, until it reached the windows and overflowed onto the street. The daughter ran to her father's arms, and burst into tears. Those, my dear people, were the happy cries you heard a few moments ago, and mistook for the cries of a punished child.

(*Everyone applauds and laughs.*)

SILK MERCHANT: Well done, old man! You've surpassed yourself!

FLOWER GIRL: That's the best tale you've told yet!

MILLER (*bowing*): I thank you.

NEWCOMER (*rushing to* MARY ANN): Is this true?

MARY ANN: I—

MILLER (*warningly*): Speak up, Daughter!

MARY ANN (*frightened*): Yes, it's true!

NEWCOMER: You touch the spinning wheel and produce gold?

MARY ANN: I—

MILLER: Speak up, daughter!

MARY ANN: Yes, it's true!

NEWCOMER: Quickly, tell me your name!

MARY ANN: Yes, it's true! I mean—Mary Ann!

NEWCOMER (*twirling her off her feet*): Mary Ann, you shall be famous! Which way to the King? (*He starts off in the wrong direction.*) Oh yes, it's through those gates, isn't it? Oh, how wonderful this is! Better than King Midas and the Golden Touch! (*He rushes through the palace gates.*)

HO-HUM (*in slow wonder*): I can't believe it. We've been invaded! (*He dashes after the* NEWCOMER.)

FLOWER GIRL (*excitedly*): He's believed the miller's story, and is going to tell the King that Mary Ann can spin gold. Everyone shall be beheaded!

(*The townspeople run to the gates and peer through.* MARY ANN *and the* MILLER *are left in the center of the square.*)

MARY ANN (*sinking to the ground*): Oh, Papa, what have you done? Papa, Papa, what have you done?

CURTAIN.

SCENE 2

The palace throne room. Three thrones decked with bright fabrics and jewels sit directly in the center of the stage. One is smaller than the others. A golden hairbrush and mirror lie on the arm of one of the larger thrones. The NEWCOMER hurries in, looks about him excitedly, and runs off the other side. After a brief pause, HO-HUM rushes in. He halts abruptly, and turns to the audience.

HO-HUM (*panting*): Which way did he go? (*He casts an anxious look behind him.*) You see, if the King finds him here, there will be trouble. No one is supposed to invade the palace. It's unheard of! (*In a confidential whisper.*) Besides, Mary Ann can't really spin gold, and we shall all be in trouble for disturbing the King with false rumors! (*He cups his hand to his ear.*) Oh, oh. I think the royal family is coming. Let me tell you about them quickly. First, of course, there is a king, and then a queen. They are attended by a jester and a maidie, respectively, and they have a handsome, intelligent son, who reads all the time. As for the King, he sleeps all the time; and the Queen—eats all the time; and the Jester and Maidie—well, they *flirt* all the time. And that is the court in its entirety. (*A trumpet is heard.*) I must hide! (*He rushes to the curtains, and hides behind them, peeking out from time to time during the scene.*)

(*Another note from the trumpet, and the* JESTER *and* MAIDIE *enter, followed by the* KING *and* QUEEN—*who carries a box of chocolates, and nibbles on them occasionally, licking her fingers. Behind them come the* PRINCE, *his nose in a book. The* JESTER *and* MAIDIE *kneel as the royal family seat themselves. The* KING *immediately falls asleep on the* QUEEN'S *shoulder. The* QUEEN *eats. The* PRINCE *reads. The* JESTER *and the* MAIDIE *tiptoe downstage, where they do a flirtatious little pantomime, ending with the* JESTER *on his knee and the* MAIDIE *giggling behind her hand.*)

QUEEN: Maidie! Come here and do my hair!

(MAIDIE *obediently flits behind the throne and begins to brush the* QUEEN'S *hair with the golden brush. Occasionally the* QUEEN'S *crown slips down over one eye during the brushing, and* MAIDIE *promptly adjusts it.*)

KING (*waking*): Jester! Jester! Come, come, don't dawdle.

JESTER: Yes, Your Majesty! (*He runs to the* KING *and kneels, waiting for a command.*)

KING: Well, well, don't dawdle. Don't dawdle.

JESTER (*puzzled*): Yes, but what do you want me to do, Your Majesty?

(MAIDIE *giggles behind her hand at this, but stops at a stern look from the* QUEEN.)

KING: Oh yes, that's right. Of course. I want you to shine my shoes, please. (MAIDIE *and* JESTER *cast a lovelorn look at each other.*) And DON'T DAWDLE! (*As the* JESTER *shines his shoes he falls asleep, even though the* QUEEN *is talking to him.*)

QUEEN: My dear, prices are dreadful today. I was just saying to Maidie yesterday, "How dreadful prices are today," I said. Didn't I, Maidie? (MAIDIE, *looking at the* JESTER *again, doesn't hear.*) Didn't I, Maidie? (*There is still no answer.*) MAIDIE! (*The* KING *wakes up.*)

MAIDIE: Oh yes, yes. Most certainly, Your Majesty, most certainly.

QUEEN (*as the* KING *goes back to sleep*): And I said to her, "Maidie, it's dreadful—"

MAIDIE (*eagerly*): Oh yes, indeed! No question about it, Your Majesty!

QUEEN: Hush up! "It's dreadful," I said. "Why, a ruby isn't a ruby any more. It's worth only half its value. It takes nineteen rubies to buy a castle of gold today, and last month it only took eight. Why, it's inflation," I said. And, my dear— MY DEAR! (*The* KING *wakens.*) Couldn't you find a way to get us more gold?

KING: That again! No, no, my dear, how often must I—

QUEEN: But there must be a—

KING: No, no, my—

QUEEN: But, I'm sure—

(*The* NEWCOMER *rushes in and falls to his knees.*)

NEWCOMER: Your Highness, Your Highness!

(*Everyone draws in breath sharply. The* QUEEN *is the first to regain composure.*)

QUEEN: Scoot!

JESTER, MAIDIE, AND PRINCE: Scoot!

KING: Yes, yes, scoot! (*The* NEWCOMER *starts to crawl out.*) Wait! Who are you? What do you mean by coming into the Royal Throne Room? (*To the others, in a loud whisper:*) Maybe I should behead him, what do you think?

NEWCOMER: No, no! Forgive me, Your Majesty, but I have great news!

KING (*drawing his finger across his throat*): It had better be!

ALL (*doing the same*): Yes, it had better be!

NEWCOMER: You know the miller who lives in the little cottage off the village square?

KING: Yes.

NEWCOMER: He has a daughter—

PRINCE (*closing his book with a bang*): Is she pretty?

NEWCOMER (*bowing*): Very pretty, Your Highness!

PRINCE: Her hair?

NEWCOMER: Light brown, Your Highness!

PRINCE: Her lips?

NEWCOMER: Ruby red, Your Highness!

PRINCE: Go on!

NEWCOMER: And this little daughter, Mary Ann by name—

PRINCE (*musing*): Mary Ann—

NEWCOMER: Has a great and beautiful talent! She can, Your Highness, put on the distaff of her spinning wheel nothing but straw and—I swear I speak truth—with several deft strokes turn this straw into—into *gold*, Your Highness!

(*There is awed silence. Then suddenly the throne room becomes a mass of excited whispers.*)

KING: Silence! Are you certain?

NEWCOMER: Absolutely, Your Majesty!

KING: Very well, bring her here. If your story is true, there will be great rejoicing. The bells will sound on the winds, and the people will dance in the streets to them. If not, there will be trouble! (*All look at the* NEWCOMER, *drawing their fingers across their throats.*) Now, run and get her!

(*The* NEWCOMER, *worried by the threat, hesitates.*)

JESTER (*with a farcical kick*): Scoot!

ALL: Yes, scoot, scoot!

(*The* NEWCOMER *runs off, bowing. The* JESTER *returns to shining the* KING's *shoes. The* KING *sleeps. The* QUEEN *eats. The* PRINCE *reads. And* MAIDIE *brushes the* QUEEN's *hair, trying not to let the crown fall over her eyes, as—*

THE CURTAIN FALLS.)

ACT 2

An anteroom in the palace. A spinning wheel is placed before a large window, which looks out over the palace grounds. MAIDIE is found kneeling at the wheel, busily readying straw. HO-HUM stands, chewing an apple, and watching her in a melancholy way.

MAIDIE (*sitting back*): There! The spinning wheel is ready! The straw is of the best . . . came straight from the King's own stables. Certainly such royal straw will weave far better gold than that poor miller's straw she has been using, don't you think?

HO-HUM (*abstractedly*): The old man weaves a story; Mary Ann hangs on to life by a lonely thread. (*He touches the thread sadly.*)

MAIDIE: Now what is all that about?

HO-HUM (*pacing back and forth*): Something must be done.

MAIDIE: Done about what? What in the world has happened to you, Ho-Hum? You used to be as lazy and nonchalant as the King. (*She looks behind her quickly after she says this.*) I wouldn't know you any more if you weren't chewing that apple.

HO-HUM: I know. This business has ruined my personality. I worry constantly. I can't even yawn any more. (*He tries to yawn, but his mouth stays open in a wide circle, and won't shut. MAIDIE runs to him and closes his mouth with her fingers.*) There, you see?

MAIDIE: Yes, it's dreadful. (*In a whisper.*) You mean you worry that Mary Ann can't really spin straw into gold? (HO-HUM *nods miserably.* MAIDIE *claps her hand over her mouth in horror.*) Everyone will be beheaded! The Newcomer, the miller, Mary Ann, and maybe even— (*She looks at him meaningfully.*)

Ho-Hum (*quickly*): Say no more! (*He paces to the window.*) Here she comes!

(MARY ANN *is seen passing the window. She stops for a moment to blow her nose into a large handkerchief.*)

MAIDIE (*beginning to cry*): How sad!

Ho-Hum: How tragic! (*He starts to yawn, but gets stuck again.* MAIDIE *runs to help him.*)

MARY ANN (*entering*): I passed the Prince in the garden. What a handsome boy—but quite strange! He was reading a book, and when he saw me he slammed it shut, threw it to the ground, and cried, "*You* are much better!"

MAIDIE: The King has given him permission to marry you after you have filled the room with gold.

MARY ANN (*sinking to the stool beside the wheel*): That's the last straw! (*Then, upon seeing the distaff of straw:*) Oh! (*She cries into her handkerchief.*)

MAIDIE (*putting her arms around her*): There, there, we'll think of something—something!

(RUMPELSTILTSKIN, *crouched over a little cane, his long coat dragging on the ground, taps on the window.*)

RUMPELSTILTSKIN (*in a queer, cracked little voice*):
> Let me in.
> Let me in.
> Open the window
> And let me in.

(MARY ANN *and* MAIDIE *jump back, astonished. They stare at him.*)

MAIDIE: What is it? Is it human?

MARY ANN: It's a little dwarf!

MAIDIE (*wringing her hands*): Pixies, pixies! We're being haunted!

MARY ANN: Nonsense! Let him in. Maybe he can help us.

HO-HUM: But perhaps he's one of the King's spies.

MARY ANN: Well, the only way to tell is to let him in. If he's a spy, he certainly is a small one.

RUMPELSTILTSKIN: Let me in.

Let me in.

Open the window

And let me in.

(MAIDIE *runs behind* MARY ANN *as* HO-HUM *opens the window.* RUMPELSTILTSKIN *enters, and stands, smiling secretly, watching* MARY ANN.)

MARY ANN: Well, close the window behind you. Don't be impolite. (RUMPELSTILTSKIN *obeys, chuckling to himself.*) Are you a spy sent by the King to find out if I can really spin gold?

RUMPELSTILTSKIN (*in his queer little voice*):

Spies are thieves.

Spies are vandals.

Spies live only on royal scandals.

Me, a spy? Never, never! (*He hobbles toward her.*) Never, never, my dear!

MARY ANN: Then who are you?

RUMPELSTILTSKIN: That is a secret for you to discover. But you are Mary Ann, the miller's daughter. Am I right?

MARY ANN (*in wonder*): How did you know?

RUMPELSTILTSKIN: That is of no consequence to the plot. (*He hobbles closer, peering at her.*) What's this I see on your cheek? Could it be a raindrop, which, landing upon such a dainty resting place, could not bring itself to depart? Or could it be a teardrop instead?

MARY ANN: Yes, a tear!

RUMPELSTILTSKIN: All the world seems dreary and cold,

Mary Ann can't spin straw into gold.

Am I right? (*All three stand in amazement.*) Surprised, aren't you? But now comes the greatest feat of them all. Just watch! (*With a funny little two-step he arrives at the wheel and sits on the stool. Next he taps his cane three times upon the floor, closes his eyes, and recites, in a singsong voice:*)

> Start with six; then add Y;
> Stir in a piece of cherry pie.
> Subtract from it a smallish sneeze,
> One black bat, and a slice of cheese.
> Multiply a witch's tooth.
> Swallow hard, and think of Ruth.
> Turn the whole thing inside out,
> And watch a piece of gold come out.

(*He opens his eyes and looks at the spinning wheel, but nothing happens.*) Drat! It didn't work! (*Slowly.*) Ah, but wait a minute. (*He reaches into his pocket and draws out a piece of gold.*) There! I must have said something slightly wrong. I wonder what it was?

MARY ANN (*overcome*): A miracle! But who is Ruth?

RUMPELSTILTSKIN: Ruth?

MARY ANN: You said something about "think of Ruth."

RUMPELSTILTSKIN: My dear child, what earthly difference does it make? Now, let's get down to business! If you are willing to wait until I remember the rest of the poem, I will conjure up a pile of gold as tall as this room and as glistening as this castle. Of course, if I think of the magic word it will fall upon us all at once, like a landslide. Otherwise, I'm afraid it will come by bits and snatches. But one way or the other, I can do it.

(MARY ANN, MAIDIE, *and* HO-HUM *clasp hands and dance joyfully about in a circle.* RUMPELSTILTSKIN *watches them a moment, then stands and hobbles toward them, slyly.*)

RUMPELSTILTSKIN: But first, a small remuneration for an old man!

MARY ANN: Remuneration?

RUMPELSTILTSKIN: For an old scoundrel just a wee sum,
And he'll be happy till Kingdom come.
For an old scoundrel, not a wee bit,
And you'll be sorry—sorry of it!

MARY ANN (*looking at herself helplessly*): But what have
I to give?

MAIDIE (*excitedly*): Your ring! How about your ring?

RUMPELSTILTSKIN: Ah, yes, your ring.

MARY ANN: Of course. My ring! (*She takes off her ring,
and gives it to him.*)

(RUMPELSTILTSKIN *two-steps happily back to the stool, taps
his cane three times on the floor, closes his eyes, and recites.*)

RUMPELSTILTSKIN: Scratch your tummy,
Rub your nose.
Breathe in deeply,
Wriggle your toes.
Stand up once,
Sit down twice.
Think of something
That rhymes with "ice."

(*A piece of gold tied to a string is descending from the ceiling.*)

MARY ANN: There it comes. There it comes.

(*She runs over and takes the gold in her hand.* RUMPEL-
STILTSKIN *gives her the other piece.*)

HO-HUM: You'd better recite the third verse in a hurry.
We're using up the day.

RUMPELSTILTSKIN (*slyly*):
Here's the best thing you've ever heard—
I've just thought of the magic word!

MARY ANN: You mean the one you say to bring the gold
all at once, like a landslide?

MAIDIE: How wonderful! Whatever is it?

(RUMPELSTILTSKIN *closes his eyes and thinks.*)

MARY ANN (*after a moment*): You haven't forgotten it so quickly?

RUMPELSTILTSKIN (*opening one eye and looking at her*): I am just thinking! (*He closes his eye again.*)

HO-HUM (*irritably*): Thinking about what?

RUMPELSTILTSKIN (*standing*): About another remuneration.

MARY ANN: I really haven't anything else—except—except my necklace. (*She unclasps it and hands it to him sadly.*)

RUMPELSTILTSKIN (*looking at it*): Hmmm. Very nice. (*He pockets it with the ring.*) However, not enough!

MARY ANN: But I tell you, I haven't anything else.

RUMPELSTILTSKIN: Oh, but you have. You have. (*Limping toward her.*) I am an old man, and all my life I have wanted a little baby.

(MAIDIE *gasps.*)

MARY ANN: A—baby?

RUMPELSTILTSKIN: Is this really much to ask?
 Making gold is such a task!
 If my request you will deny,
 I'll leave you here and let *you* try!

MARY ANN (*helplessly*): But where can I find a baby?

RUMPELSTILTSKIN: Don't find one. *Have* one. You'll marry the Prince. Give me your first-born!

MAIDIE: Heir to the throne! The King won't stand for it!

RUMPELSTILTSKIN (*impressively*): Very well, I'll give you one more choice. Now listen carefully. If by the time one year has passed, you can think of my name, I will leave the child here. If not—

MARY ANN: And I suppose you have a terribly complicated name! (*Hiding her face in her hands.*) Very well. Say the word. I have no choice.

RUMPELSTILTSKIN (*moves front center*): Everybody move back! Close your eyes, and hold your ears. You mustn't hear the word, or you'll be able to make gold any time you have the urge.

(MARY ANN, HO-HUM, *and* MAIDIE *move as directed.* RUMPELSTILTSKIN *mouths a very long word, raising his arms slowly. Suddenly, thunder and lightning. The lights go out. A great noise is heard:* S-W-O-O-S-H!)

MARY ANN, HO-HUM, AND MAIDIE (*in the darkness*): It's gold—gold—GOLD!

CURTAIN.

ACT 3

SCENE 1

Almost a year has passed. The scene is an opening in a forest where a quaint little house with a broken stovepipe is leaning against a tree. Next to the door of the house stand two brightly colored fairy wings, an artist's stool, some paint jars, and brushes. RUMPELSTILTSKIN stands over a simmering pot in the center of the opening. He drops powder into the brew and stirs it with a long ladle.

RUMPELSTILTSKIN: Simmering, shimmering bright red dye—
Two more days and I shall fly
Over the cottages, over the town,
Straight to the palace, where I'll come down—
Down with a thump on the palace lawn.
Then past the guard with the lazy yawn,
On past the Princess, sweet and mild,
Into the room of the newborn child!

(*He tastes the liquid in the pot, and shakes his head.*) This most certainly isn't red! It looks like red, but it doesn't *taste* like red. (*He goes to the wings and dabs some paint on them.*) They'll never run without red. Let's see, perhaps if I add some tomato juice! (*He exits into the cottage.*)

(*After a moment,* HO-HUM *enters wearily, carrying a large scroll. He is followed by the* JESTER *and* MAIDIE.)

HO-HUM: At last—a house!

MAIDIE: And something is cooking in that pot! (*She runs to it and sniffs, then turns away, holding her nose.*) Phew!

JESTER (*sitting and rubbing his feet*): I wouldn't be fussy at this point.

MAIDIE: Well, you would be if you had a whiff of *that!* (*Tugging at her nose.*) I wonder if I shall ever smell again!

HO-HUM (*sitting next to the* JESTER): Well, whose turn is it to collect the names?

JESTER: Not mine! I did it last time. Don't we have enough now? Just look at the size of that scroll.

HO-HUM: This will be our last stop, and then we can safely say—

JESTER AND MAIDIE (*as if they've heard this before*): "We've covered the entire Kingdom!" We know!

HO-HUM: Don't forget, if the dwarf's name isn't somewhere on the list, we'll lose an heir to the throne.

MAIDIE: And Princess Mary Ann will lose her baby! Very well, I'll do it. (*As she moves toward the door of the cottage, she suddenly hesitates.*) I don't know whether I should! There's something about this place I don't like—something in the air—

HO-HUM: It's only the smell from that pot.

JESTER: Hold your nose, and go ahead.

MAIDIE (*holding her nose*): Very well. (*She goes to the door, and raises her hand to knock.*)

RUMPELSTILTSKIN (*from within the house*):
>Today I brew,
>Tomorrow I bake,
>The next day Mary Ann's child I take—

MAIDIE (*jumping back*): Did you hear that?

HO-HUM: I've heard that voice before!

RUMPELSTILTSKIN: For little dreams this royal dame
>That Rumpelstiltskin is my name.

HO-HUM: The dwarf! My stars, we've found him! (*Turning excitedly to the* JESTER.) What did he say his name was?

JESTER (*rising, excitedly*): *Rumple* something or other.

MAIDIE (*who has been listening with her ear against the door*): Watch out! He's coming.

(*They run behind the corner of the house and peek out as* RUMPELSTILTSKIN *appears and hobbles to the pot. He carries a large bottle of tomato juice.*)

RUMPELSTILTSKIN (*pouring the juice into the pot*): There! That's much redder. Now let me see, what was that poem I was saying a minute ago?

MAIDIE (*behind him, in a high, eerie voice*): "Today I brew—"

RUMPELSTILTSKIN: That's it. "Today I brew." (*He looks at the sky.*) Thank you, Ruth! (MAIDIE, HO-HUM *and the* JESTER *dissolve in silent laughter behind him.*)

>Today I brew,
>Tomorrow I bake,
>The next day Mary Ann's child I take.
>For little dreams this royal dame
>That Rumpelstiltskin is my name.

(*Chuckling to himself, he stirs the concoction in the pot.*) MAIDIE, HO-HUM *and the* JESTER *whisper excitedly behind him, and then tiptoe off into the forest.* (*Peering off:*) What was that? Who's there? That you, Ruth? (*There is silence.*

Shrugging his shoulders, he returns to the fairy wings and begins to dab paint on them, as—

THE CURTAIN FALLS.)

SCENE 2

The market place. The crowd is busily decorating a platform, on which are placed two large thrones and two smaller ones. Gay streamers and balloons deck the stage. Ho-Hum leans against the gates, chewing an apple, and watching the activity.

NEWCOMER (*entering*): What's this? A festival of some kind?

Ho-Hum: Haven't you heard? Today the dwarf will come to kidnap the baby!

NEWCOMER: Does that call for a celebration?

Ho-Hum: Certainly! Everybody knows the story, and they can't wait to see his face when Mary Ann tells him his name. It will be a great joke. (*He yawns.*) Have you noticed how well I can yawn again? (*A trumpet sounds off stage. Pushing open the gates:*) Here they come! Kneel everybody!

(*The crowd kneels as the* JESTER *and* MAIDIE *run on and take their positions behind the two larger thrones. Then comes the* KING, *pushing a baby carriage. He is followed by the* PRINCE *and* MARY ANN, *who enter hand in hand. Finally comes the* QUEEN, *escorted by the* MILLER, *and nibbling from her perennial box of chocolates. The royal family seat themselves, and the* KING *promptly falls asleep.*)

MAIDIE (*handing the large scroll to* MARY ANN): He should be here any minute, Your Highness! You'd better practice.

MARY ANN: Let me see. "Today I brew, Tomorrow I bake—"

(*There is a loud thud off stage.*)

Ho-Hum (*peering through the gates*): There he is! (*He giggles.*) Sitting on the ground with his eyes closed, muttering to himself.

(*The crowd runs to the gates. The* KING *wakes up.*)

KING: What's happening?

QUEEN: Hush up, dear. Go back to sleep.

MARY ANN (*standing*): I don't know why, but I feel nervous. What's he doing now?

FLOWER GIRL: He's taking his wings off and getting up. Now he's hobbling toward the window. He's peeking in! Watch out, he's looking this way! (*The crowd ducks behind the gateposts.*)

Ho-Hum: Everybody look nonchalant now.

(*The crowd assumes bored positions.* RUMPELSTILTSKIN *appears, carrying his wings, tucked under one arm.*)

RUMPELSTILTSKIN (*putting down his cane, and rubbing his extremities*): What a bump! I knew that paint never tasted red enough. (*He looks about.*) Greetings, everyone.

Ho-Hum (*yawning*): Hello.

RUMPELSTILTSKIN: This is a merry gathering. (*To* MARY ANN:) I have come for the baby. (*Seeing the carriage.*) Ah, there he is! (*He hobbles to it and peers in.*) What a silly contraption to keep him in. When he's mine, I shall let him crawl about on the grass and snow where he belongs. That's the way *I* was brought up.

MILLER: And look what happened!

RUMPELSTILTSKIN: Pardon me?

MILLER (*bowing*): That's a very interesting theory, sir! And when he's old enough, you will teach him his "magic spelling"?

RUMPELSTILTSKIN: Well, on with the business! I suppose you wish to ask me some names, Mary Ann?

MARY ANN (*opening the scroll*): Indeed I do!

RUMPELSTILTSKIN (*sitting on the platform, leaning on his cane*): Proceed!

MARY ANN (*standing, reads*):
>Ham, Sam,
>Arnie, Barnie,
>Will, Bill,
>Edward Milarney?

(RUMPELSTILTSKIN *chuckles. The crowd begins to laugh with him. He stops suddenly.*)

RUMPELSTILTSKIN (*sternly*): Continue!

MARY ANN: Ebeneezer, Alakasqueezer,
>Istanbul, or simply the "Sneezer"?

(*Again* RUMPELSTILTSKIN *laughs and the crowd joins him.*)

RUMPELSTILTSKIN (*stops laughing suddenly, scowls at the crowd*): Stop that! You have nothing to laugh about! (*The people stop laughing out loud, but continue to snicker behind their hands.*)

MARY ANN: Ignatius?

RUMPELSTILTSKIN (*standing*): Ye gracious!

MARY ANN (*quickly*): Or what about this? "Today I brew, tomorrow I bake—

HO-HUM, MAIDIE and JESTER join her: "The next day Mary Ann's child I take—

EVERYONE: "For little dreams this royal dame
>That *Rumpelstiltskin* is my name!"

(*For a moment* RUMPELSTILTSKIN *stands still, staring into space, speechless. Then he gives way to rage.*)

RUMPELSTILTSKIN (*screaming*): Some witch told you that! (*He screams and starts dancing a dance of fury.*) Drat it, Mary Ann, you win! Rumpelstiltskin never goes back on his word, so you may keep your baby. (*He dances to the side of the stage by the palace gates and begins to put on his wings.*) Are you ready, Ruth? I'm coming home now—empty-handed Hooptidle, hooptidle, up in the sky—this magical mumble will help me to fly. (*He pushes against an imaginary weight with all his might, but it makes him slowly drop to his knees.*) No, no. *Up*, not down. Fly—*fly!* Oh dear, now I won't be home till tomorrow. (*Exits, crawling.*)

(*With merry shouts the people join hands and dance in a circle.* Ho-Hum *saunters toward the audience.*)

Ho-Hum: That is the end of the story. Rumpelstiltskin kept his word and never returned again. In fact, Mary Ann, the Prince, and the baby lived (*he stands back and opens his arms*) *happily ever after!* And now, if you will be kind enough to applaud, here are the actors in our play!

(*Everyone on stage moves forward and bows, as—*

THE CURTAIN FALLS.)

Around the World
in Eighty Days

Adapted by

PAMELA PRINCE WALKER

Cast (*in order of appearance*)

PHILEAS FOGG
TWO GENTLEMEN OF THE REFORM CLUB
PASSEPARTOUT
RALPH
BEGGAR WOMAN
FIX
INDIAN GUIDE
BRAHMIN PRIESTS AND NATIVES
AOUDA
JAPANESE DANCERS AND ACROBATS
JAPANESE THEATER MANAGER
SAN FRANCISCO CITIZENS
CAMERFIELD
MANDIBOY
PORTER
TRAIN PASSENGERS
CONDUCTOR
AMERICAN INDIANS
NEW YORK SAILORS AND DOCK WORKERS
CUSTOMS OFFICER

SHIP PASSENGERS
NEWSBOY
LONDONERS
MINISTER

TO THE DIRECTOR:

This play should be produced by junior high school children—that is, seventh, eighth, and ninth graders. It is too advanced for grade school students to enact, although they may enjoy watching it.

Although it calls for a large cast of characters, many of the small roles and all of the crowd scenes may be enacted by the same children with a change of costume.

Since there are seven different settings, the director should be careful to keep them extremely simple. A bright blue backdrop is suggested with one or two pieces of gay cardboard scenery against it, these cardboard pieces changed with each scene to suggest each different country. Costumes may also be handled by clothing the children in a simple, basic piece and changing the hats and accessories to designate the different countries.

Suggestions for making the elephant and the balloon are included in the script.

ACT 1

SCENE 1

A London street in 1872. A sign, stage right, bears the words "Saville Row." Near it stands a frame doorway with "Number 7" printed in neat, conservative letters above it. Next to the doorway stands a small lamppost. A row of flowers leads down the walk to the street. Stage left is another doorway with the sign "Reform Club" hanging over it. A similar row of flowers leads from this doorway to the street.

Behind the doorway marked "Number 7" we see a comfortable chair, a side table, and a standing lamp. In the chair sits MR. PHILEAS FOGG, reading his paper. MR. FOGG, we will see later, is a quiet, bespectacled man with a reserved expression which sometimes becomes quite comically deadpan. As of now, we cannot see him at all; he is hidden behind his paper, the *London Times*.

Behind the doorway of the Reform Club we see a bridge table and four leather chairs. Two of the chairs are occupied by GENTLEMEN of the Club. Like MR. FOGG they are just now concealed behind copies of the *London Times*.

PASSEPARTOUT enters from stage left and starts down the street. He is a gay Frenchman in a gay costume, consisting of a bright shirt, a bright bow tie, a derby with a bright ribbon—and a mustache. As he reaches center stage, he stops to look at his watch—a large silver one, which he draws from his pocket.

PASSEPARTOUT (*turning to the audience*): Nineteen minutes after eleven A.M.—exactly. (*He holds up the watch proudly.*) A family watch passed down from my great great grandfather. It doesn't vary five minutes in the year. I am Passepartout (*bows and tips his hat*)—a Parisien from Paris. I am a *très gai* Parisien. My life has been full of adventure. I have been (*counting on his fingers*) an acrobat, a tumbler, a clown, and even (*wrinkles his nose in distaste*)—an actor. *Oui,* I have been a little of everything. Now, I choose to become Passepartout, the servant! (*He bows once more, tipping his hat.*) Why, you ask, a mere servant—this *très gai* Parisien of Paris, this man of many talents? Because, my friends, I am tired. (*He mops his brow with a checkered handkerchief.*) *Oui,* tired! I am growing older every day. Now I will settle down and rest. It has come to my attention that a man lives upon this street (*he draws a small card from his pocket*)—Saville Row—who is prim, prudent, and practical. He keeps time meticulously (*proudly showing his watch*). He is very dull. In fact, he never leaves Saville Row, but spends his time between his home at Number Seven and the Reform Club. And this man wants a servant. (*Blissfully:*) Ah, I see ahead a path of quiet virtue—a path which lies between (*pointing*) Number Seven, Saville Row—and the Reform Club. No more excitement; no more adventure. At last there will be peace for Passepartout. (*Consulting his card.*) Mr. Phileas Fogg. Number Seven, Saville Row. Between eleven and eleven-thirty A.M. (*Consulting his watch.*) I must hurry!

(*He hurries to Number Seven and lifts his hand to knock, just as* FOGG *emerges. They collide.* PASSEPARTOUT *drops his watch,* FOGG *his black umbrella. As they bend to retrieve them they bump heads. They rise, tip hats, bend again, and once more bump heads.* PASSEPARTOUT *becomes greatly agitated, but* FOGG *leans upon his umbrella and faces the audience with no expression whatsoever.*)

PASSEPARTOUT (*flustered*): Mr. Phileas Fogg?

FOGG: Correct.

PASSEPARTOUT: Number Seven, Saville Row? (FOGG *simply raises his umbrella and points it to the sign over the doorway without in any way changing his expression or moving his head.*) Between eleven and eleven-thirty this morning?

FOGG (*coolly consulting his own watch*): The time, sir?

PASSEPARTOUT (*fumbling for his silver watch, dropping and retrieving it quickly*): Exactly twenty-two minutes after eleven, sir!

FOGG (*casually*): You are fast—

PASSEPARTOUT: Pardon me, sir, it is impossible—

FOGG: You are two minutes too fast. No matter. It's

enough to mention the error. Now from this moment, twenty-nine minutes after eleven A.M., this Wednesday, the second of October, you are in my service.

PASSEPARTOUT (*happily*): Yes, sir! (*Bows low.*)

(FOGG *tips his hat slightly and proceeds down the street to the Reform Club.* PASSEPARTOUT *snaps his fingers, does a quick dance step, hurries into Number Seven, collapses into the armchair, and falls asleep.* FOGG *walks methodically, counting his steps. Arriving at the Reform Club he takes out a small notebook and writes in it, muttering, "Left foot, twenty-seven steps, right foot—time—" A gentleman enters from stage left and approaches the door of the Club.*)

FOGG: Ah, Ralph, how goes the robbery?

RALPH (*clapping him on the back as they enter the Club*): Phileas, my man, I believe we may put our hands on the robber. Skillful detectives, you know, particularly this man Fix—

FOGG: How much did the bank lose exactly?

RALPH (*sighing heavily as they seat themselves at the card table*): Fifty-five thousand pounds! (*The* TWO GENTLEMEN *who have hitherto been hidden behind their papers now put them down and whistle in unison: "Whew!"*) But we have an elegant description of the man! Elegant!

FOGG (*shuffling cards*): Quite a gentleman, I hear.

RALPH (*enthusiastically*): Prim, prudent, and proper. Medium height, quiet appearance, carries a black umbrella, bespectacled— (*He pauses. All eyes are on* FOGG.) Why, Phileas, quite like you! (*All three chuckle merrily.*)

FOGG (*dealing*): Quite!

1ST GENTLEMAN: I maintain that the chances are in favor of the thief.

RALPH: Never! As I say, we have this description— (*A pause. All look at* FOGG. RALPH *continues, less convinced.*) Besides, where would he go? No country is safe for him.

1st Gentleman: Oh, I don't know that. The world is big enough.

Fogg (*playing his hand*): It was once.

2nd Gentleman: What do you mean, "once"? Has the world grown smaller?

Fogg (*coolly*): It is 1872, sir.

1st Gentleman: Just because one can go round it in three months—

Fogg: In eighty days!

Ralph: That is true, gentlemen. Eighty days is an estimate made by—

1st Gentleman (*beginning to be angry*): Does this estimate take into account bad weather, shipwrecks, accidents?

Fogg: Eighty days.

1st Gentleman: Hindus who pull up the rails?

Fogg: Eighty days.

1st Gentleman: Indians who stop the trains and scalp the passengers?

Fogg: Eighty days. (*He has not raised his eyes from the cards.*)

1st Gentleman (*very excited*): Practically speaking, Mr. Fogg—

Ralph: Yes, Phileas. Practically speaking—

Fogg (*not raising his voice*): Eighty days.

1st Gentleman (*leaping to his feet*): I'd like to see you do it in eighty days!

Fogg (*not raising his eyes*): Be so kind as to play, sir.

1st Gentleman: I repeat, Mr. Fogg, I should like to see you—

2nd Gentleman (*rising*): Yes, I should like to see—

Ralph (*rising*): Gentlemen, gentlemen!

Fogg: Very well, I shall do so! (*A silence falls.*) At your expense, gentlemen. (*They sink to their chairs, staring at him.*)

1ST GENTLEMAN (*weakly*): I would wager four thousand—

FOGG: I have a deposit of twenty thousand pounds at Barings, gentlemen. It is yours if I do not arrive at the Reform Club, after my journey, at the precise moment of (*consults his watch*)—let me see, the train leaves for Dover at a quarter before nine—

RALPH (*jumping up, very nearly knocking over the table*): But, my dear Phileas, surely you don't intend to leave this evening?

FOGG: I do, sir!

1ST GENTLEMAN (*rising*): But, my dear Phile—Mr. Fogg, you must jump mathematically from steamers to trains and from trains to steamers—

FOGG: I will jump—mathematically.

2ND GENTLEMAN (*rising*): But, my dear Phile—Mr. Fogg—

FOGG: Enough! I will wager the twenty thousand pounds. If I do not (*again consulting his watch*) arrive on the doorstep of the Reform Club on Saturday, the twenty-first of December, at exactly a quarter before nine P.M., you may proceed to Barings to collect the twenty thousand pounds. Here is a check for the amount. (*He proceeds to write out a check.*)

RALPH (*hastily*): We must suspend the game so that Mr. Fogg has time to—

GENTLEMEN: Of course, of course.

FOGG (*most unperturbed*): I am quite ready now. Diamonds are trumps. Be so good as to play, gentlemen.

(*They sit, awed. Slowly the game resumes.*

THE CURTAIN FALLS.)

SCENE 2

A sign saying "Charing Cross Railway" emerges between the curtains and stays there—suspended. A BEGGAR WOMAN in a tattered dress sits center under the sign, moaning to her-self. FOGG enters from stage left in front of the curtains, count-ing his steps. He is followed closely by Passepartout, who carries a small carpetbag, and who skitters nervously from side to side of his master—now tugging his coattails, now taking out the checkered handkerchief to mop his own brow.

PASSEPARTOUT: But, Mr. Fogg—sir—you must listen—please, sir—

FOGG (*pulling his coat away*): Be so good as to loosen your hold. You will rip my coattail.

PASSEPARTOUT: But, sir this mad adventure—

FOGG (*coolly*): The time, please?

PASSEPARTOUT (*on one knee*): But, sir—

FOGG: The time.

(PASSEPARTOUT *stands. He and* FOGG *consult their watches.*)

PASSEPARTOUT (*sighing heavily*): Twenty-seven minutes—

FOGG (*crisply*): Before nine. Good! I see you have cor-rected your timepiece. We may now proceed. (*He walks to center, counting his steps.* PASSEPARTOUT *follows dejectedly.*)

BEGGAR WOMAN (*moaning*): Alms. Alms.

FOGG (*takes the carpetbag from* PASSEPARTOUT, *draws from it a large number of bills, hands them to the* BEGGAR WOMAN, *as* PASSEPARTOUT *watches in amazement*): Here, my good woman. I'm glad that I met you. (*He tips his hat to her and exits between the curtains.*)

PASSEPARTOUT (*turning to the audience, mopping his brow*): Ah, my friends, what's the use? My quiet life—my life of peace—pfft! (*Snapping his fingers.*) Like that! I am the serv-ant of a madman, a madman who gives fortunes to beggars (*he points to the woman, then begins to weep*), a madman who makes bets, a madman who wishes to take me around the world in eighty days! (*Blowing his nose loudly, he exits through the curtains.*)

(*The* BEGGAR WOMAN *rushes off, happily counting her money. The sign saying "Charing Cross Railway" disappears.*

FIX, *the detective, enters from between the curtains. He is very much a detective, from the cap pulled low over his eye to the trench coat, into the pockets of which he digs his hands. He even wears dark glasses, but takes these off upon seeing the audience.*)

FIX (*peering right, then left; in a loud whisper*): I am Fix— the detective. (*He flashes his badge.*) You heard about me at the Reform Club—remember? I am the one who is hired to find the robber who stole the money from Ralph's bank. And I can do it if anyone can! You see, I am a very good detective: sly (*he looks about in what he considers a sly manner*), quick-witted (*he points to his head*), quick on the draw (*he tries to draw his hand from his pocket, but it gets caught and he must struggle to loosen it*), tough (*he curls his lip*), brave (*a loud crash backstage and he nearly jumps out of his coat. Regaining composure:*) I think, friends, I have my man. Listen to this! (*He draws from his pocket a slip of paper and reads.*) The criminal is described as follows: prim, prudent, proper. (*He glances knowingly at the audience.*) Medium height, quiet appearance, *carries* a *black umbrella.* (*He nods wisely.*) *Bespectacled*— (FOGG *enters stage right in front of the curtain, followed by an anxious* PASSEPARTOUT, *carrying the carpetbag.* FIX *quickly hides between the curtains and peeks out after them as they cross the stage,* FOGG *counting his steps, and exit stage left.* FIX *emerges.*) Right you are! Mr. Phileas Fogg! Why, I ask you, would such a man—a quiet man, a man of habit—leave his home, his country, his England—to travel around the world? Why? (*He chuckles meanly.*) Because he has stolen fifty-five thousand pounds from a bank—that's why—and I, Fix, the detective (*again he flashes his badge*), will catch him. I have followed him to Suez, to Bombay, and I will follow him across the world if need be— (*Sadly.*) You see, I have sent to London for a warrant for his arrest. It is on the way, mind you, but it is not as fast as Mr. Fogg. Wherever he goes, the warrant follows— but too late. (*More sadly.*) It always arrives too late. (*More happily.*) Still, it will catch up with us one of these days, and meantime I will follow him, if it means—if it means crossing India upon an elephant! Follow him I will to the ends of the earth. (*Lowering his voice, dramatically.*) For I am Fix, the detective! (*He winks at the audience, then, pulling his cap over his eye and his coat collar up about his neck, he sidles off after* FOGG, *whistling in what he hopes is a careless manner.*)

CURTAIN.

SCENE 3

The curtains open upon a scene in India—a simple scene with a blue sky for background, and some low bushes downstage right. Indeed, the only way we know it is India is because, almost immediately upon opening, there enters from stage right an elephant. This elephant, upon close observance, does not seem a very frightening animal. In fact, if we draw very near, it strongly resembles a tall cart on wheels, pulled by two children, both cart and children being covered with some sort of gray material. But let's look again. It certainly has the head of an elephant, trunk, big ears, and all. And that is surely an elephant's tail. Yes, we may be certain—an elephant it is, and upon its back, in great style, rides our own PHILEAS FOGG, accompanied by PASSEPARTOUT and an INDIAN GUIDE. The elephant stops, and the three passengers climb down. They appear rather warm, and PASSEPARTOUT is rubbing his backside vigorously, but otherwise we see they have fared nicely. Seating themselves next to the bushes, they begin to take large sums of money from the carpetbag. Finally they arrive at three sandwiches, which they proceed to devour hungrily.

PASSEPARTOUT (*with his mouth full*): How many more miles to Allahabad?

GUIDE: About forty, sirrah.

FOGG: And you are quite certain there is a railway from there to Calcutta?

GUIDE: Yes, sirrah. Oh, a fine railway—

PASSEPARTOUT (*grimly*): Let us hope it is better than the last one.

FOGG (*taking out his notebook*): We can still make connections—mathematically, if we finish our sandwiches and proceed without delay. (*All three fall to eating rapidly.*)

PASSEPARTOUT (*more grimly*): Now we travel on elephants. I ask you, Mr. Fogg, how does one travel around the world in eighty days—on an elephant? What will happen next? What *will* happen next?

(*A tom-tom beat resounds loudly from off left.* PASSEPARTOUT *and the* GUIDE *jump to their feet and look excitedly about.* FOGG *continues to eat his sandwich.*)

GUIDE (*in great agitation*): Brahmins!

PASSEPARTOUT (*knees shaking*): B-brahmins?

GUIDE: A band of cruel natives who live in these parts.

PASSEPARTOUT (*nearly fainting*): C-cruel band of natives?

GUIDE (*peering off in the direction of the sound*): It will not be good for us to be found here.

(PASSEPARTOUT *heads toward the elephant.*)

FOGG: Have we time to finish our sandwiches?

GUIDE: It would be most unwise, sirrah.

FOGG: Very well. (*He stands up coolly, wraps the sandwich in paper, and begins to put the bankrolls back into the carpetbag.*)

(PASSEPARTOUT *is already scrambling onto the back of the*

elephant. The tom-tom beat comes nearer. The GUIDE *climbs onto the elephant, followed by the imperturbable* FOGG. *The* GUIDE *hits the elephant rather hard and cries "Ho!"—but it doesn't move. Again the* GUIDE *swats the elephant, shouting "Ho!" Still it doesn't move. The tom-tom beat is very near now.*)

PASSEPARTOUT: *Mon dieu! Mon dieu!*

FOGG (*coolly*): Let us all hit the elephant together and cry "Ho!" Ready, now. One, two, three—

ALL THREE: (*slapping, kicking the elephant*) Ho!

FOGG: Again!

ALL THREE: Ho!

FOGG: Again!

ALL THREE: Ho! (*The drum is almost deafening by now.*)

PASSEPARTOUT (*loudly*): Ho, ho, ho!

GUIDE: Very strange! The animal has always obeyed before.

FOGG (*nodding*): Very strange!

PASSEPARTOUT (*wildy*): Ho, ho, ho, ho, ho!

GUIDE: No use. We must take refuge.

PASSEPARTOUT (*tumbling off the elephant*): Refuge—refuge — (*He dashes wildly about the stage.*)

FOGG (*climbing down deliberately*): I believe the only refuge in sight is this underbrush. (*He kneels behind the bushes.*)

PASSEPARTOUT *and the* GUIDE *rush to the bushes and fall behind them just in time. From stage left enter the* BRAHMINS. *First come the priests, faces painted, and clothed in long, brilliant robes. They chant an eerie psalm, accompanying themselves on drum, tambourine, and cymbal. Four richly clothed natives follow, drawing a brightly colored cart. On the cart is an ugly statue with a comical expression upon its green face—its eyes popping, its tongue sticking out. More priests follow the cart. Two of them lead a beautiful Indian girl. She wears a glittering golden dress, sparkling jewelry, a soft muslin robe. When she first appears she seems to be trying to pull away from her captors, but as she crosses the stage and exits on the other side with the procession, she subsides into gentle weeping. Three heads pop over the bushes as the last of the* BRAHMINS *exit.* PASSEPARTOUT *and the* GUIDE *are wide-eyed.* FOGG *munches his sandwich calmly, as they watch the procession depart. The chant ceases, followed by the tom-tom beat.*)

FOGG: Guide, what were those barbarians going to do with that young lady?

GUIDE: Kill her, sirrah.

PASSEPARTOUT: K-k-kill her?

FOGG: Do you know this of a certainty?

GUIDE: Did you see the statue they were pulling ahead of her?

FOGG: I did.

GUIDE: Kali—the goddess of love and death!

FOGG: I see.

PASSEPARTOUT (*hopefully*): But if it's a statue of love and death, perhaps this is to be a love ceremony.

FOGG: Nonsense! When people wish to make love they do not do it with such fanfare. They go off quietly somewhere.

GUIDE: Not the Brahmins, sirrah. They perform a similar ceremony for the marriages.

PASSEPARTOUT: And drag that hideous statue about? I'd hate to turn around after kissing the bride and come face to face with that!

FOGG: How do you know this is not the marriage ceremony, Guide?

GUIDE: The young girl is well-known in these parts. She is Aouda, most beautiful and most sweet daughter of a rich merchant.

FOGG: What is her story?

GUIDE: There is not much to tell. Aouda's family married her to an old man against her wishes. Now the man has died and the Brahmins will kill her, according to custom.

PASSEPARTOUT (*angrily*): Pleasant little custom!

GUIDE: The fakirs—

PASSEPARTOUT: You can say that once again. Fakers! Scoundrels! Wretches!

FOGG: Quiet! I must think. (*He consults his watch, thinks. Then, quietly:*) We will save her. (PASSEPARTOUT *and the* GUIDE *jump up in astonishment.*)

GUIDE (*quickly*): But how—?

PASSEPARTOUT (*falling to his knees*): Master, please consider—

GUIDE: Impossible—

PASSEPARTOUT: We must reach Calcutta by—

FOGG: We will save her! (*He says this with such an air of assurance that the others fall silent.*)

GUIDE (*slowly*): Sirrah, if I may say so, you are a man of heart.

FOGG (*putting his watch away*): Sometimes, when I have the time.

PASSEPARTOUT (*miserably*): But how? How?

FOGG: One of you take a look over there and tell me if you can still see the barbarians.

(*The* GUIDE *hurries to stage right and peers off.*)

GUIDE: Yes, sirrah. They seem to be sleeping, as is their custom before—

FOGG: Excellent! This is my golden opportunity. (*He takes a last bite of his sandwich, puts it neatly away, and walks to right, followed by a wild-eyed* PASSEPARTOUT.)

PASSEPARTOUT (*tugging* FOGG's *coattails*): Please, please, Mr. Fogg—

FOGG: Release me at once, sir. (PASSEPARTOUT *releases the coat and falls back.*)

PASSEPARTOUT (*weakly*): How? How?

FOGG: While they sleep, I shall simply take my place behind the statue of—

GUIDE: Kali.

FOGG: Quite right—Kali. Then with a frightful roar I shall lift the statue off its feet. These barbarians are sentimental creatures and will be, I am assured, quite taken back to see the statue rise above them. With the statue before me I shall move to Aouda, release her, and carry her off to safety. (*He turns to exit.*)

PASSEPARTOUT (*grabbing the coattails again*): Master, I cannot let you do this. I will go instead.

FOGG: You?

PASSEPARTOUT: Remember, I have been (*counting on his fingers*) an actor, a clown, a tumbler and—an acrobat! Surely I am more agile than you and can run more quickly, if necessary.

FOGG (*thinking*): It will not be necessary to run. But you *are* strong. (*He feels* PASSEPARTOUT's *muscles.*) The statue may be heavy.

PASSEPARTOUT: It is settled, then. I shall do it. (*He turns to the audience.*) What next, I ask you? (*He exits grimly.*)

FOGG (*calling after him*): Do not run! It will make them suspicious!

(*He returns to his sandwich, as the* GUIDE *peers anxiously after* PASSEPARTOUT.)

(*A pause. From off stage comes a great shout. This is* PASSEPARTOUT. *It is followed by cries of fear from the natives.*)

GUIDE (*excitedly*): He has the statue!

FOGG (*quietly*): What are the barbarians up to?

GUIDE: They have fallen to their knees.

FOGG: As I thought. (*He resumes eating.*)

GUIDE (*nearly distraught with excitement*): He is moving to Aouda.

FOGG: Not running, I trust?

GUIDE: No, walking.

FOGG: Good.

GUIDE: Though, not too slowly! (*A pause.*) Ahh! (*Falls to his knees and holds his head, rocking back and forth, moaning.*)

FOGG (*looking up*): What has happened?

GUIDE: He cannot undo the ropes she is tied with. He is fumbling. (*Muttering from off stage.*) They grow suspicious. Ah!

FOGG (*joining the* GUIDE, *peering off with his hand shading his eyes*): It appears I must rescue them both. (*He begins to exit, but the* GUIDE *detains him by his coattails.*) What? You too? (*Pulling loose.*)

GUIDE: No, sirrah. Just look! (*He points off.*)

FOGG (*looking*): Good, he has freed her. (*The* GUIDE *jumps up and down happily, tugging* FOGG's *coattails. More cries of fear from the natives.*) Here he comes. (*Calling.*) Walk slowly! Do not hurry! (*Turns to the* GUIDE; *casually:*) Come, my good man, to the elephant. Let us hope it will move for us this time.

(FOGG *and the* GUIDE *climb on the elephant.* PASSEPARTOUT *rushes onstage, carrying* AOUDA, *who has quite collapsed from the excitement. He is very much out of breath.*)

FOGG: I told you not to run.

PASSEPARTOUT (*lifting her up*): Here, take her quickly. (*The tom-tom starts again. A few wild cries come from very near.*) They have caught on. Quickly, quickly!

(FOGG *takes* AOUDA, *who falls unconscious upon his shoulder.* PASSEPARTOUT *climbs up behind, facing backward toward the oncoming natives. There was sufficient room for three on the elephant, which apparently is a baby one, but four are a bit of a crowd. In fact,* PASSEPARTOUT *nearly falls off the back end, but manages to stay on by holding onto the tail for dear life.)*

FOGG: All together now. One, two, three—

ALL THREE: Ho! (*The elephant begins to move.*)

FOGG: One, two, three—

ALL: Ho! (*The elephant goes a little faster.*)

FOGG: One, two, three—

ALL: Ho! (*The elephant tears across the stage.*)

FOGG: One, two, three—

ALL (*offstage by now*): Ho! (*The natives dash on and look about wildly. Then with a cry they rush off again in the wrong direction. A long pause.*)

FOGG (*in the distance*): One, two, three—

ALL: (*far, far away*): Ho!

(*Another pause. From stage right enters another elephant, which bears a remarkable resemblance to Fogg's. On its back sits none other than* FIX, *his expression set, his hat pulled down, his sun-glasses on, slouched low in his seat. The elephant crosses the stage deliberately and exits as—*

THE CURTAIN FALLS.)

SCENE 4

The stage of a Japanese theater in Yokohama. A colorful backdrop of Japanese design and several Oriental screens comprise the entire setting. In the center of the stage, sitting cross-legged with his head in his hands, is a Japanese man in vivid Oriental attire. He is wearing a long rubber nose and heavy rouge. He holds in one hand a triangle; raising his hand slowly, he strikes this once or twice. Then he shakes his head sadly. Presently his nose commences to itch, and he begins to try to scratch it. This soon proves futile and he removes the rubber nose. It is PASSEPARTOUT.

PASSEPARTOUT (*scratching his nose*): *Oui*, it is I, Passepartout! You wonder what I do here in Yokohama in this Japanese theater—in this Japanese costume? You say the last time you saw me I was racing through India on the back of an elephant? (*Scrambles to his feet and comes down to the footlights.*) It is a miserable story! Miserable! (*Sits in front of the footlights, dangling his feet off the stage.*) Have you met Fix, the detective? You have. Then you know he has been following Mr. Fogg around the world, hoping to arrest him for bank robbery as soon as the warrant arrives from England. (*In disgust.*) Bank robbery! Phileas Fogg! It is an outrage! A madman, yes, but never a bank robber. (*Takes off his turban and dabs his eyes with it.*) I warn you, it is a miserable story. We arrived in Calcutta in plenty of time to catch the steamer here to Yokohama. In fact, we thought we had nearly a day to wait. Mr. Fogg took Aouda to a hotel so she could rest after her strenuous experience. I went to the wharf to look at the ships. (*By this time, he is on his feet, enacting all that happened.*) There I found that we were mistaken and our ship was to sail not a full day later, *but in a few hours.* (*Claps his hand to his head in horror.*) I began to run as fast as I could (*Jog-trots rapidly in place*) to tell Mr. Fogg. Then whop! (*Stops suddenly and nearly falls over.*) I bump into this little man with the cap over his eye and the collar about his neck. (*Pulls the turban down and the Japanese costume up, imitating* FIX.) It is Fix, the detective. (*Flashes an imaginary badge, as* FIX *would.*) He tells me Mr. Fogg is a bank robber, so I bop him in the nose. (*Bops the air with his fist.*) Then I bop him again. (*Does so.*) And again and again. (PASSEPARTOUT *is quite carried away, dancing about the stage, bopping the imaginary* FIX.) Finally the fight is over (*mops his brow*) and Mr. Fix and I retire to the nearest smoking house to make amends over a glass of beverage. (*Pretends to sit and sip a drink. He makes a funny face, as if he has tasted something unpleasant. He spits out the imaginary drink, and topples over upon the floor, unconscious. Immediately he stops acting and jumps up, facing the audience angrily.*) That is the last thing I remember. Fix has fixed everything, including my drink. I wake up on the ship to Yokohama. Poor Mr. Fogg and Aouda have not made connections, for I have not told them the ship sails early. (*Looks at his watch.*) It is now November fourteenth. Mr. Fogg has only thirty-seven more days to go around the world. He will never make it—never. (*Beginning to weep.*) Phileas Fogg has lost his wager! If I ever see that Fix I shall fix him for once and for all. (*Grows wild-eyed.*) "Fix," I'll say, "Fix—" (*Begins to dance about and bop the air again.*)

(*A troupe of Japanese players enter behind him and take places. They include three lovely dancing girls, a pair of tumblers, several magicians who twirl batons and wave handkerchiefs throughout the scene, and two musicians—one carrying a gong, the other a cymbal. The men in the troupe all wear long rubber noses, similar to Passepartout's. A dancing girl runs to Passepartout and whispers in his ear.*)

PASSEPARTOUT (*to audience*): In the meantime, regardless how sad he feels, a man must work. (*Shrugging his shoulders, he takes up his triangle, puts on his nose, and stands with the other musicians.*) The show will begin!

(*The three dancing girls move to the front and execute a graceful dance with their fans, accompanied by the gong, cymbal, and triangle. Each time PASSEPARTOUT hits the triangle he makes a wry face to the audience, as much as to say, "See what a man must do to work!" Throughout the dance the tumblers and magicians perform, and the stage resembles a three-ring Oriental circus. Their dance over, the girls step aside and the men come to the center where they begin to form a pyramid. It is a business demanding careful balance. PASSEPARTOUT is on the bottom tier. Just as the last man pre-*

pares to climb to the top, there is a loud crash off stage. The pyramid totters dangerously, as all the participants look off to see what has happened. Then with a shout PASSEPARTOUT *jumps into the air. Down comes the pyramid, to the cries and shrieks of the dancing girls. The stage is in utter confusion.*)

PASSEPARTOUT (*rushing to the side of the stage*): Mr. Fogg! Mr. Fogg! Aouda! Mr. Fogg!

(*In his excitement he knocks over a large screen. Everyone becomes immobile, staring at the revealed spectacle:* FOGG *and* AOUDA—*in a balloon! The balloon is a simple one, consisting of a large clothes basket, in which the couple are standing, with the ropes attached to it extending upward to a multicolored beach umbrella. If the beach umbrella is turned upside down and partially hidden by the upper curtain, the effect is of a very gay and colorful balloon. The ropes are covered with crepe-paper streamers. Undoubtedly* FOGG *has made it himself. His expression, however, reveals nothing as he stands in the basket with his arm about the beautiful* AOUDA.)

PASSEPARTOUT: Mr. Fogg! Mr. Fogg, sir! I am so glad—*so* glad—but how did you arrive?

FOGG (*pointing with his umbrella*): Through the ceiling. (*A little man rushes on and begins to talk to* FOGG *in rapid Japanese. He flings his arms about wildly, from time to time pointing to the ceiling. To* PASSEPARTOUT:) What is he saying?

PASSEPARTOUT (*shrugging his shoulders*): How should I know! He is the theater manager.

FOGG: Undoubtedly he wants me to pay for his ceiling. (*Pointing his umbrella at the* MANAGER.) Sir, you should take a lesson from the English on the construction of solid foundations. If this building had been made of brownstone, instead of paper— (*The* MANAGER *begins to gyrate once again.*) Very well, sir. (*Draws a substantial roll of bills from his car-*

petbag, and hands them to the MANAGER, *who exits happily.*)

PASSEPARTOUT (*still looking at the balloon*): But *how*, sir—?

FOGG: Never mind the past. On to the future. What time is it? (*He and* PASSEPARTOUT *consult their watches.*)

FOGG AND PASSEPARTOUT (*together*): Sixteen minutes before nine o'clock, the fourteenth of November.

PASSEPARTOUT: Thirty-seven more days!

FOGG: And one minute!

PASSEPARTOUT: Can we do it, sir?

FOGG: Hop in. The ship leaves for San Francisco within the hour, and we must not lose our minute.

(PASSEPARTOUT *leaps into the basket, as* FOGG *begins to turn the wheel. Everyone watches with fascination. But nothing happens.* AOUDA *holds out* FOGG'S *umbrella to catch the breeze. Nothing happens. The players surround the balloon, puff out their cheeks, and blow as hard as they can. Still nothing happens.*)

PASSEPARTOUT (*grimly*): Just like the elephant!

FOGG: No, no, good people. Blowing will not help at all. We had difficulty starting from the beach in Calcutta, and there we were in a typhoon.

PASSEPARTOUT (*gasping*): Typhoon!

(*The players look at each other with raised eyebrows. Typhoon? Ah yes, now they understand. They nod their heads happily and begin to blow even harder.*)

FOGG: No, no. Here Aouda, give me that. It will not help. (*He takes the umbrella, patting* AOUDA'S *cheek as he does so.*) There is nothing left but to walk to the steamer, as speedily as we may. (*He helps* AOUDA *out of the basket, and all three hurry down the steps to the center aisle of the theater.*)

PASSEPARTOUT (*as they exit up center aisle*): Hurry sir. Hurry. There may still be time. Thirty-seven days. Can we do it, sir? Can we do it?

(*The* THEATER MANAGER *rushes onstage and beckons anx-*

iously to the players. They start to perform again—without the triangle. The curtains begin to close. Apparently this does not please the manager, for he becomes very voluble indeed, throwing his arms about and shouting at someone off stage, obviously the curtain-puller. He even holds onto one curtain, trying to stop it. They continue to close, however, and at last, just before he is lost from view, he clasps one hand to his head in defeat and with the other holds up a sign that says

"INTERMISSION".)

ACT 2

SCENE 1

In front of the railway station in San Francisco. A frame doorway with a sign hanging over it, saying "Union Pacific Railway," stands center stage. People pass by along the street, including businessmen in tall silk hats and carrying canes, a flower vendor, an Indian, and several young girls in long dresses. PASSEPARTOUT rushes on from one side of the stage, looking at his watch anxiously, dropping it, retrieving it. FIX rushes on from the other. They collide at the station door.

PASSEPARTOUT: You!

FIX: You!

(PASSEPARTOUT *takes a long swing and bops* FIX *in the nose. The detective lands on the street. He sits up, rubbing his nose.* PASSEPARTOUT *pulls him to his feet and begins to swing again, but* FIX *catches his arm.*)

FIX: Stop! Let me explain.

PASSEPARTOUT: Explain nothing. You would arrest Mr. Fogg as a bank robber. You would detain him in Calcutta, make him miss his connections, make him lose his wager—

FIX: Wait! I cannot detain him, or arrest him here. The warrant for his arrest is not effective on American soil. (*Waves a paper in* PASSEPARTOUT's *face.*)

PASSEPARTOUT: Is that the warrant?

FIX: It is! (PASSEPARTOUT *swings back, but once again* FIX *catches his arm.*) Wait, wait! I tell you I am on your side now. I am willing to do everything in my power to aid Mr. Fogg in reaching England within eighty days.

PASSEPARTOUT: Eighteen days! Only eighteen! *Mon dieu!* (*Mops his brow and looks at his watch.*)

FIX: Within eighteen days. I shall be at your service from now until then, and will help in every way I can. (*To audience.*) Once he is on British soil again, I shall arrest him— the scoundrel!

PASSEPARTOUT (*looking at him doubtfully*): You now agree that Mr. Fogg is no thief?

FIX (*nodding energetically*): Indeed! Indeed!

PASSEPARTOUT: And that he is a forthright, honest gentleman who travels around the world on a wager?

FIX: Oh, yes indeed!

PASSEPARTOUT: A madman, yes, but a bank robber, never!

FIX (*emphatically*): Never! (*Winks at the audience.*)

PASSEPARTOUT (*stroking his chin and looking at* FIX; *suddenly*): What made you change your mind?

FIX: I—er—uh—

(*He is saved from having to answer by a loud din: shouts of "Hurrah for Camerfield!" from one side and "Hurrah for Mandiboy!" from the other. The noise becomes louder and two crowds, waving banners and flags and shaking their fists violently, enter from either side. On the shoulders of two of the agitators we see* AOUDA, *now in English costume, with a chic little veiled hat and a wide skirt. She is looking about in puzzlement.* FOGG *follows close behind, prodding the men with his umbrella.*)

FOGG: I have asked you to release the lady, sirs, and I shall be forced to take concrete action if you do not do so.

FIRST MAN (*Imitating* FOGG's *accent*): Fawced to take concrete action! (*The crowd roars with laughter.*) And wot concrete action do you propose to take, sir? (FOGG *reaches up with his umbrella and soundly raps both men on the head. The crowd roars again, as the two men drop* AOUDA, *who straightens her hat and skirts primly.*)

CROWD ONE (*pushing a gentleman in tall silk hat forward*): Hurrah for Camerfield! We want Camerfield!

CROWD TWO (*pushing a similar gentleman forward from their midst*): Hurrah for Mandiboy! Speech! Speech!

CAMERFIELD: Friends! Patriots! Americans! (*A roar of approval from his supporters. Hisses and boos from the Mandiboys.*)

MANDIBOY: We are gathered together—

CAMERFIELD: On this occasion—

MANDIBOY: To commemorate—

CAMERFIELD: To elect—

(*Someone from the crowd jeers loudly, "Quiet Camerfield! Let a* real *speaker speak!" Cries of "Hear! Hear!"*)

MANDIBOY: Friends!

CAMERFIELD: Patriots!

MANDIBOY: Americans! (*Loud shouts from both sides.*)

FOGG (*stepping forward and raising his umbrella*): If you will kindly move away from the station door and allow us to enter, we may still make our connections and reach England by the appointed day.

(FOGG *looks at his watch. Shouts and laughter from the crowd. "Elect the Englishman!" "We want the Englishman!" The crowds start forward but* CAMERFIELD *and* MANDIBOY *stop them.*)

CAMERFIELD: Good people—

MANDIBOY: Fine people—

BOTH: Americans! (*The noise subsides.*)

CAMERFIELD (*to* MANDIBOY): Were we not scheduled to speak in the park?

MANDIBOY (*nodding*): On the bandstand!

BOTH: To the park! (*They march off, followed by their crowds.*)

(*A red-capped porter enters, wheeling a cart of suitcases.*)

PASSEPARTOUT (*to* FOGG): Hurry, sir! Please hurry. Only eighteen more days.

FOGG: Yes, indeed. We were detained by the mob. Porter, were those people electing someone for office?

PORTER: Yes suh.

FOGG: Very high office, I suppose.

PORTER: Yes suh.

FOGG: General-in-chief, perhaps? (PASSEPARTOUT *is pulling him through the station door by the coattail.*)

PORTER: Oh, no suh.

FOGG: Prime minister, then?

PORTER: Oh, no suh. Justice of the peace! (FOGG *exits through the doorway backwards, pulled by* PASSEPARTOUT *and* FIX. AOUDA *trips quickly along behind them.*)

PORTER (*shaking his head*): An' they say us Americans is allus in a hurry! (*Giggling.*) These Britishans, don' they beat all? Man! (*Still shaking his head, he exits through the station door with a loud giggle.*)

CURTAIN.

SCENE 2

On a train. Several passengers sit, reading newspapers and sleeping quietly. FOGG, FIX, and AOUDA sit at a small table playing cards. After a moment PASSEPARTOUT hurries in, mopping his brow.

FIX: Where have you been, Passepartout? It is your play.

PASSEPARTOUT (*sitting, taking up his cards*): Up in the front, talking to the engineer. Such a *slow* fellow. I explained we must reach London in twelve days and asked if there was no way to go faster.

FIX: What did he say?

PASSEPARTOUT: He said he was from Texas.

FIX: Texas? What does that have to do with it? (PASSEPARTOUT shrugs.)

FOGG: It is against the nature of a Texan to hurry.

PASSEPARTOUT (*in exasperation*): Then, *why* must we have a Texan for an engineer?

FOGG (*calmly*): It is your play.

(PASSEPARTOUT *sorts his cards, shakily. Then he flings them upon the table, rises, and paces up and down the aisle.*)

PASSEPARTOUT: I should like to get out and push! (*There is a sudden jolt, which wakens the sleeping passengers and throws* PASSEPARTOUT *to the floor. Rising and hurrying to the window:*) We have stopped!

CONDUCTOR (*entering*): Will everyone please listen carefully. We have encountered a small problem.

PASSEPARTOUT: Problem, problem. What problem?

CONDUCTOR: The bridge which sits a few feet in front of us over a tall precipice is—no longer there.

PASSEPARTOUT: No longer there. Where did it go?

CONDUCTOR: Probably blown up by the Indians.

PASSEPARTOUT: Indi-Indi-Indians?

FOGG (*smiling in spite of himself*): American Brahmins.

PASSEPARTOUT: Yes, sir, I s-see. But if the bridge is no longer there, how do we reach the other side?

FOGG: Precisely the problem. (*Peering out the window.*) It seems a rather narrow precipice.

CONDUCTOR: Narrow—but deep!

FOGG: Nor more than a few inches across. Perhaps if we

all held on tightly and the engineer backed up a ways and gave it steam—

FIX: We could tear right across at full speed—

PASSEPARTOUT (*delightedly*): Without falling at all! (*All three shake hands with glee. Then they shake hands with* AOUDA, *who smiles happily.*) We may still make it, Mr. Fogg.

CONDUCTOR: We will take a vote.

PASSEPARTOUT: Vote. Vote. Why a vote?

CONDUCTOR (*firmly*): This is the American democracy, sir. We will take a vote. All in favor of crossing the precipice at full speed, raise your hands.

(FOGG, FIX, PASSEPARTOUT, *and* AOUDA *raise their hands without hesitation. The rest of the passengers do not move.*)

PASSEPARTOUT (*jumping upon the seat*): Cowards! Mice! What have you to lose? Only your lives! If we do not reach London in twelve days we will lose twenty thousand pounds!

FIX (*to audience*): Money is as important as life to this Parisien of Paris!

PASSEPARTOUT (*eloquently*): I beg of you, my friends, be brave! We have brawled with Brahmins, ballooned with typhoons, pugilized with politicians. What is a little precipice to us? We have crossed the Suez, the Indian Ocean, the Pacific!

CONDUCTOR: For twenty thousand pounds?

FOGG (*quietly*): For honor, my dear sir, for honor.

PASSEPARTOUT: Of course, for honor! Do you think we will stop now with only twelve more days to go? Give it all up? Give up twenty thousand pounds for a few weak-kneed Indians?

(*An Indian in full war dress jumps through the window and topples* PASSEPARTOUT *to the floor. Screams from the passengers.* FOGG *lifts his umbrella and quietly raps the Indian on the head. The Indian turns, bewildered.* FOGG *raps him again. The Indian falls unconscious.*)

AOUDA: Another, sir, another!

(*Two more Indians leap through the window and engage* FOGG. *Meanwhile, several more are sneaking down the aisle toward him.* FOGG *takes them all on with his umbrella, and one by one the natives fall to the floor, unconscious.* AOUDA *finishes the job each time with a sound bop of the carpetbag.* FIX *then carts them off stage, one by one. Each time he exits we hear a loud "plunk" off stage and* FIX *then re-enters, rubbing his hands together in satisfaction. When all the Indians have been thus removed,* FOGG *jumps on the seat.*)

FOGG (*coolly*): Any more?

(*One of the Indians begins to crawl groggily back down the aisle, but* AOUDA *taps him lightly with the carpetbag and he falls back in a swoon.* FIX *removes him, panting.*)

FIX: That's all, sir. (*He collapses.*)

FOGG: Very well. (*To the* CONDUCTOR.) Let us proceed.

CONDUCTOR (*thunderstruck*): But—but the vote—

FOGG (*glancing about and seeing that all the passengers have fainted, even* PASSEPARTOUT *and* FIX): By all means!

CONDUCTOR (*weakly*): All in favor of crossing the precipice at full speed—

(FOGG *and* AOUDA *raise their hands quickly. The* CONDUCTOR *looks about at the unconscious passengers, then exits, muttering to himself.* FOGG *and* AOUDA *sit, smiling at each other, holding hands. There is another jolt. The passengers,* FIX, *and* PASSEPARTOUT *awaken.*)

PASSEPARTOUT (*hurrying to the window*): We are going backward. Backward! Only twelve days and now we go backward!

(*Another jolt and everyone holds tightly to his seat. With a loud toot and a chug, chug, chug, the train rushes forward. We hear the wind whistle by. The passengers hold on for dear life.*)

FOGG: We are going forward now.

FIX: No doubt about it.

PASSEPARTOUT: Over the precipice.

AOUDA: Hold tight.

PASSEPARTOUT: Whee!

AOUDA: Whee!

FIX: Whee!

FOGG: Whee! (*They look out the window.*) Here we go. Hold onto your hats! (*Chug, chug, chug. The wind roars by. The train whistle blows. The passengers hold onto their hats —and their breaths. A suspenseful pause. Suddenly everyone rises and cheers loudly.* "We made it!" "We're across!"

FOGG (*settling back, picking up his cards*): On to London.

FIX, AOUDA, AND PASSEPARTOUT (*cheering*): On to London! (*They sit and take up their cards.*)

FOGG (*to* PASSEPARTOUT): Your play.

PASSEPARTOUT (*happily*): *Ah, oui!*

(*They begin to play. The other passengers sit back. Some pick up their papers. Others fall asleep. The* CONDUCTOR *enters, and comes down the aisle. At center stage he holds up a sign saying "Time passes" and exits. He returns immediately with another sign saying "More time passes" and exits again.*)

FOGG (*to* FIX, *calmly*): You trumped my ace.

FIX (*smugly*): Indeed I did.

FOGG: Are you out of spades?

FIX (*looking at his hand*): Oh, dear!

PASSEPARTOUT: You mean we must start all over?

(*The* CONDUCTOR *enters, crosses, holds up a sign saying "Eleven more days." He turns to the passengers and calls:* "All out for New York!" *Exits.*)

PASSEPARTOUT (*jumping up*): New York! New York!

FOGG (*consulting his watch*): We have only ten minutes to cross the city if we wish to catch the steamer.

PASSEPARTOUT: Ten minutes! *Mon dieu!*

AOUDA (*reaching for the carpetbag*): My hat.

(*There is a jolt.*)

PASSEPARTOUT: Hurry, hurry.

AOUDA (*putting on her hat; to* FOGG): You like?

FOGG (*patting her cheek*): Very nice, my dear.

PASSEPARTOUT (*grabbing the open carpetbag*): Hurry, please, hurry.

(*The money and several hats fall out of the carpetbag.*) *Mon dieu!*

FIX: Fool!

(*They all begin to cram the money and hats back into the carpetbag. The rest of the passengers exit.*)

PASSEPARTOUT: Ten minutes and she thinks of hats. Women! (AOUDA *begins to cry gently.*)

FIX (*hurriedly piling money in the bag*): Enough, idiot! You spilled the money, not Aouda.

PASSEPARTOUT: But, if she hadn't reached for her hat—

FOGG: It is a woman's nature. (*Fixes the hat carefully on* AOUDA's *head.*) Very nice, my dear. (AOUDA *begins to smile through her tears.*)

AOUDA (*to* FIX): You like?

FIX: Charming!

AOUDA (*to* PASSEPARTOUT, *hesitating, but hopeful*): You like?

PASSEPARTOUT: Elegant, elegant! (*At this,* AOUDA *smiles so winningly,* PASSEPARTOUT *warms in spite of himself. He blushes and squirms about.*) Aw! (*Another jolt, and a loud train whistle.*) We're starting! *Mon dieu!* (*All four rush down the aisle and exit,* FOGG *backwards, as before, being pulled by the coattails. A pause. Suddenly, the hat blows back in and lands jauntily in the aisle, followed by* PASSEPARTOUT.)

PASSEPARTOUT (*grabbing the hat and hurrying out*): Women!

CURTAIN.

SCENE 3

The wharves of New York. The bow of a ship, a gangplank, and the blue sky comprise the setting. Sailors swagger by. A uniformed CUSTOMS OFFICER stands by the gangplank. Several men are loading cartons onto a pushcart. The hat blows on from stage right and lands cockily on one of these men.

DOCK WORKER: What in the—?

PASSEPARTOUT (*rushing on*): Women! (*He starts for the hat.* AOUDA *enters.*)

AOUDA: Oh, my beautiful hat!

(FOGG *and* FIX *enter.* PASSEPARTOUT *rescues the hat and hands it to* AOUDA *with a low bow.*)

AOUDA (*curtsying*): Thank you, sir.

PASSEPARTOUT (*melting at her smile*): Aw!

FOGG (*to* DOCK WORKER): Could you kindly tell me if that ship is the *China,* leaving for Liverpool within the hour?

DOCK WORKER: Yup! (*He returns to his work.*)

FOGG: We have arrived in time. Let us each check our identification, passport, ticket, and photo.

(FOGG *and* FIX *draw papers from their pockets.* PASSEPARTOUT *opens the carpetbag and searches for his.* AOUDA *retires to the side of the stage, turns her back to the audience, lifts her skirts, and draws hers from her stocking.*)

FOGG: Identification.

PASSEPARTOUT (*checking his papers*): Identification.

FOGG: Passport.

PASSEPARTOUT: Passport.

FOGG: Ticket.

PASSEPARTOUT: Ticket.

FOGG: Photo.

PASSEPARTOUT: Photo. (*Begins to put away his papers. Suddenly he stops.*) Photo? (*Leafs hastily through the papers, finds the photo, and stares at it. His hands begin to shake. Then his knees begin to knock together. He takes out his checkered handkerchief and mops his brow. Weakly:)* Mr. Fogg, sir—

FIX: What now, fool?

FOGG *(impassively)*: You have lost your photo?

PASSEPARTOUT: Not exactly, sir, I—

(He hands the photo to FOGG who stares at it a moment, then hands it to AOUDA. AOUDA claps her hand over her mouth and passes it to FIX.)

FIX *(furiously)*: Idiot!

PASSEPARTOUT *(taking the photo)*: I don't see how such a thing could have happened!

FOGG: It has, however. We will see what may be done. *(Turns and marches to the CUSTOMS OFFICER at the gangplank, followed by the others.)*

OFFICER *(politely)*: Your papers, sir?

FOGG: Certainly. *(Hands the officer his papers.)*

OFFICER: Very good. Proceed. *(FOGG passes him and stands on the gangplank. To FIX:)* Your papers?—Proceed. *(FIX moves to the gangplank. To AOUDA:)* Your papers, ma'am? —You may proceed. *(AOUDA joins the others on the gangplank. All three hold their breaths as PASSEPARTOUT moves forward, his knees quite out of control. With a long look at PASSEPARTOUT's knees:)* Your papers, please? *(PASSEPARTOUT looks desperately at FOGG, who regards him stoically.)* Your papers, if you please? *(PASSEPARTOUT tries to speak, but his teeth chatter.)* If I may kindly see your papers, sir! *(PASSEPARTOUT gives up his papers, and turns away, downcast. The OFFICER leafs through the papers. When he comes to the photo, he stares at it for a minute. Then he stares at Passepartout, who wiggles about and looks at his feet.)* I am afraid you have handed me the wrong photo, sir. *(Smiles and shows the picture to the miserable PASSEPARTOUT.)* You see?

PASSEPARTOUT (*glumly*): I see.

OFFICER: Have you another?

PASSEPARTOUT (*more glumly*): That is the one.

OFFICER: But, sir—

PASSEPARTOUT: *C'est ça!* That is it! (*Shrugs.*)

OFFICER: But sir, this is the picture of an American Indian!

(*The* DOCK WORKERS *turn and stare at* PASSEPARTOUT, *who immediately tries to look like an American Indian. He gets a wild look in his eye, sneaks about in a circle, and even emits a halfhearted war whoop. Then he looks hopefully at the men, who continue to stare at him.*)

PASSEPARTOUT (*weakly*): An Indian?

FOGG (*crisply*): Perhaps I can explain, officer. We have just crossed the continent upon a train, you understand. On the way we were attacked by a ferocious band of savages. This gentleman came to our defense.

(PASSEPARTOUT *nods enthusiastically and begins to dance about the stage, bopping imaginary Indians.*)

AOUDA: It was he who rescued us.

FOGG: It was he who saved our lives.

FIX (*with a certain amount of sarcasm*): Whatever would we have done without him?

(PASSEPARTOUT *puts his thumbs in his lapels and paces about importantly.*)

FOGG: When the battle was over, we noticed our carpetbag had spilled forth its contents upon the aisle of the train. (PASSEPARTOUT *obligingly dumps the contents of the carpetbag before the astonished* OFFICER.) Among the contents were this gentleman's papers. You understand. In our haste to collect the articles we must have—

FIX (*his eyes upward*): Picked up the picture of an American Indian!

FOGG: Quite so.

OFFICER: Impossible! Indians don't go about taking snap-shots of one another.

(*The* DOCK WORKERS *roar with laughter.*)

PASSEPARTOUT (*angrily*): This one did.

OFFICER: I'm sorry, sir—

PASSEPARTOUT: But—

FOGG: But—

(AOUDA *slips forward and touches the* OFFICER'*s arm. She smiles benignly and points at her hat.*)

AOUDA: A new hat. You like?

OFFICER: Charming.

AOUDA (*pushing it over one eye, coquettishly*): Like so? (*The* OFFICER *begins to warm. He grins and shakes his head. She quickly pushes it over the other eye.*) Like so?

OFFICER (*gently adjusting the hat*): No, like so. (PASSEPART-OUT *begins to sneak by. The* OFFICER *chucks* AOUDA *playfully under the chin.* FOGG *reaches forward with his umbrella and prods the* OFFICER *in the ribs. Giggling, thinking it is* AOUDA): Ouch. That tickles.

FOGG (*poking him again*): Release the lady, sir!

OFFICER (*turning in time to see* PASSEPARTOUT *sneaking up the gangplank*): Stop! Stop! Stowaway!

(*He chases* PASSEPARTOUT, *who heads back down the gang-plank. About the wharves they go, followed by* FOGG, *who flourishes his umbrella. There is a sudden deafening blast of a horn. The gangplank is drawn up and disappears over the side of the ship.*)

PASSEPARTOUT (*on his knees by the contents of the carpet-bag*): Wait! Wait! I have found it! Here, look! (*Holds up the photo.*)

OFFICER (*looking at the photo, looking at the departing ship, jumping up, blowing his whistle*): Hold it, up there. Wait! There has been a mistake!

EVERYONE: Wait! Stop!

(The ship pulls farther away. The OFFICER *continues to blow his whistle. The rest wave their arms and shout frantically. To no avail. The ship disappears. A pause.)*

FOGG *(throwing off his coat):* We will swim for it!

(All turn to him in amazement. Opening his umbrella and holding it over his head, FOGG *prepares to jump.)*

CURTAIN.

ACT 3

SCENE 1

The docks of Liverpool. Stage right is a ship's bow and gangplank. Stage left is a barred doorway with a sign saying "Liverpool Custom House." A bench sits center stage. Passengers are descending the gangplank, greeting people who stand waiting on the wharf, and exiting in a flurry of excitement. PASSEPARTOUT comes dancing down the plank, falls upon the ground, and kisses it.

PASSEPARTOUT: England! Dear England! Home again!

(Down the plank comes FOGG *and* AOUDA, *hand in hand. They are followed by* FIX. AOUDA *looks about breathlessly.)*

AOUDA: So this is England.

FOGG: Do you like it, my dear?

AOUDA: It's lovely.

PASSEPARTOUT *(jumping to his feet, embracing* FOGG): Mr. Fogg, you are to be congratulated. You have made it, sir, you have made it.

AOUDA: And we didn't even have to swim.

FIX *(rolling his eyes up):* Thank heaven for that!

PASSEPARTOUT: The other ship came along in the nick of time. Mr. Fogg, providence has been with you.

FOGG: Providence and a cool head.

AOUDA (*laughing*): I don't know what is this providence, but the cool head (*taps* FOGG'S *head*), that much I am sure of. (*Shakes hands with* FOGG.)

FOGG (*embarrassed, consulting his watch*): We have a little over six hours in which to reach London. The train should take us six hours exactly. Let us proceed!

PASSEPARTOUT (*happily*): What more can happen? Here there are no Brahmins, no Indians to stop us. We have as good as won the wager. England! Dear England! (*Falls to kissing the ground again.*)

FOGG: Nevertheless, let us proceed! (*Takes* AOUDA'S *arm and starts across the stage,* PASSEPARTOUT *dancing happily behind him.*)

FIX (*clearing his throat*): Ahem! Phileas Fogg, Seven Saville Row, London, England! (*All three stop and turn to him, as he pushes his cap over his eye, turns his collar up, and flashes his badge.*) Scotland Yard, sir!

FOGG: Mr. Fix, we must make a train in exactly (*consults his watch*) ten minutes. If this is a joke, sir—

FIX (*trying to be very tough*): This is no joke. I have a warrant for your arrest. (*Produces the warrant.*)

PASSEPARTOUT (*gasping*): Why, you—

FOGG (*coolly*): On what grounds, sir?

FIX: Bank robbery, sir.

FOGG: I see.

PASSEPARTOUT: Why, you—

FIX (*handcuffing* FOGG, *who has not changed his expression*): I arrest you in the Queen's name.

FOGG: If you are suggesting the robbery of the Bank of England some three months ago, sir—

FIX: I am.

FOGG: In which a gentleman, by description—

FIX: By description, prim, proper, prudent, bespectacled, *and* carrying a black umbrella— (*Taps* FOGG'S *umbrella.*)

FOGG: Made off with fifty thousand pounds—

FIX: Fifty-five thousand pounds. (*Taps* FOGG's *carpetbag.*)

FOGG: Then, sir, I am not your man.

FIX: That remains to be seen. (*Starts down the street toward the Custom House with* FOGG *in tow.*)

FOGG: You understand, I am not saying this to boast, sir, but only to show you the extent of your folly. I am a very close friend of the president of said bank. He calls me Phileas.

FIX: That remains to be seen.

FOGG (*as they disappear into the Custom House*): I call him Ralph!

PASSEPARTOUT (*throwing the carpetbag upon the ground*): Why, you—

AOUDA: Oh, dear. (*Sits disconsolately upon the bench. Her lips begin to tremble.*) Oh dear!

PASSEPARTOUT (*sitting next to her*): Oh, dear, dear, dear, dear! (*They both take out their handkerchiefs and blow their noses.*)

AOUDA: And we could have made it.

PASSEPARTOUT: It's too late now.

(*A* NEWSBOY *goes by calling* "Paper! Paper! Liverpool Gazette. *Get your daily news! Paper, sir?*" PASSEPARTOUT *shakes his head sadly.* NEWSBOY *exits.*)

PASSEPARTOUT: Twenty thousand pounds—*pfft*—like that! (*Snaps his fingers.*)

AOUDA: And Mr. Fogg's honor, too—*pfft!* (*Tries to snap her fingers, but they make no sound.*)

PASSEPARTOUT: Of course, of course. His honor. (*We can tell that this is of secondary import to* PASSEPARTOUT.)

AOUDA (*suddenly*): Passepartout, you are my friend, aren't you?

PASSEPARTOUT (*taken aback*): Why, of course.

AOUDA (*clasping his hand*): My very good, loyal friend?

PASSEPARTOUT (*squirming uncomfortably*): Aw!

AOUDA (*ardently*): Then I must ask you something.

PASSEPARTOUT (*more embarrassed*): Aw! (*As* AOUDA *falls to her knees before him, jumps to his feet, frightened.*) No, no, wait a moment!

AOUDA: Just one little question?

PASSEPARTOUT (*horrified*): Please, consider—

AOUDA: When every time a girl sees a man her heart goes bump-bump-bump, like this—

PASSEPARTOUT: Please—

AOUDA: Her cheeks become pink, like this—

PASSEPARTOUT: Oh, please—

AOUDA: Her breath comes short (*gasps*), like this—

PASSEPARTOUT (*clapping his handkerchief to his forehead*): Oh, no!

AOUDA: Tell me, dear Passepartout, what is the English word for this?

PASSEPARTOUT (*collapsing upon the bench; weakly*): Rheumatic fever?

AOUDA (*sitting beside him*): Fever? I do not think so. Fever is a sickness, is it not? This thing I feel for Mr. Fogg is not a sickness.

PASSEPARTOUT: A form of the flu? Or grippe? Or—Fogg? Fogg? (*Amazed.*) You feel this bump of the heart for Mr. Fogg? (AOUDA *nods anxiously.*) Your cheeks grow pink for Mr. Fogg? (AOUDA *nods.*) Your breath comes short (*he gasps*) for Phileas Fogg? (AOUDA *nods. A smile spreads across* PASSEPARTOUT's *face.*) Well, I never!

AOUDA: What is the English word for this, Passepartout?

PASSEPARTOUT: In Paris, where I come from, the word is *amour.*

AOUDA (*thoughtfully*): Amour! And in English?

PASSEPARTOUT: In English the word is— (FIX *enters from the Custom House, his head lowered. Immediately* PASSEPARTOUT *is on his feet.*) Advance, coward, for a bop on the nose! (FIX *comes forward slowly, hanging his head.* PASSE-PARTOUT *prepares to strike him, but stops, his arm in mid-air.*) What is the matter? Are you sick?

FIX (*nodding*): Sick at heart!

AOUDA: Like me—you have rheumatic fever for Mr. Fogg.

FIX: I do not believe he did it. I am *certain* he did not do it. (*Sits on the bench.*)

PASSEPARTOUT: Of course, he did not do it.

AOUDA: Of course.

FIX (*sadly*): Of course.

PASSEPARTOUT (*clasping* FIX *by the collar, drawing him to his feet*): Then why in heaven did you arrest him?

FIX (*flashing his badge*): It was my duty. (*Takes off badge and throws it to the ground.*)

AOUDA (*rescuing the badge, pinning it back on* FIX): Oh, no. Don't do that. You are a fine policeman. Sly— (FIX *taps his head and assumes a sly expression.*)

PASSEPARTOUT: Quick on the draw— (FIX *tries to get his hand from his pocket, but gets it stuck.*)

AOUDA: Brave— (*A crash off stage. All three are startled.*)

FIX (*sitting; more melancholy than ever*): It's no use. As a detective, I am a failure.

AOUDA (*sitting beside him, patting his hand*): Don't say that.

PASSEPARTOUT (*sitting, patting his other hand*): No, don't say that.

FIX (*shaking his head*): A failure. A total failure. Perhaps I should have been a milkman. I always wanted to be a milkman.

AOUDA (*shaking her head*): It is just this—rheumatic fever we all have for Phileas Fogg!

(*The* NEWSBOY *re-enters, calling,* "Paper. Paper. Get your daily paper here. Bank robber caught. Fifty-five thousand pounds reclaimed by Bank of England. Paper, sir?" *All three shake their heads glumly. The* NEWSBOY *starts to exit. "Get your daily paper here.")*

FIX *(jumping to his feet)*: Bank robber!

PASSEPARTOUT *(jumping up beside him)*: Fifty-five thousand pounds!

(They rush after the NEWSBOY.)

FIX: Here, boy, give me that paper.

NEWSBOY: That will be one shilling, sir.

*(*FIX *pays no attention. He grabs the paper and scans it with* PASSEPARTOUT *and* AOUDA.)

FIX: Bank robber caught—

PASSEPARTOUT: Bank of England—

FIX: Three months ago—

PASSEPARTOUT: Fifty-five thousand pounds! *(They look at each other dumbfounded. Then they look at* AOUDA.)

AOUDA *(still looking at the paper)*: What a horrible-looking man! Not at all like Mr. Fogg!

(Joining hands, they rush into the Custom House. The NEWSBOY *follows them, crying, "That will be one shilling, please." But they have disappeared. Shrugging his shoulders the* NEWSBOY *turns and exits, calling, "Paper. Paper. Get your daily paper here.")*

CURTAIN.

SCENE 2

The sign saying "Charing Cross Railway" appears through the curtains and a clock strikes nine. FOGG, AOUDA, FIX and PASSEPARTOUT enter before the curtains and stand, looking at their watches.

FOGG *(crisply)*: Too late!

ALL: Too late!

FOGG: By fifteen minutes!

ALL: Fifteen minutes!

PASSEPARTOUT: If I hadn't produced that picture of the Indian—

AOUDA: If I hadn't lost my hat—

FIX (*wailing*): If I had only been a milkman!

FOGG: Never mind the past. On to the future! (*Puts out his finger.*) It looks like rain. (*Putting up his umbrella, he crosses the stage, counting his steps, and disappears. The others sadly follow him.*)

CURTAIN.

SCENE 3

Saville Row. FOGG's house and the Reform Club, as before. The same TWO GENTLEMEN sit in the Reform Club reading their newspapers. Nothing has changed. FOGG and AOUDA enter, arm in arm, under the umbrella. AOUDA carries the carpetbag.

FOGG: Well, here we are, my dear. Home!

AOUDA: Home!

FOGG: And only twenty minutes late. Not bad.

AOUDA: Not bad. (*She begins to weep.*)

FOGG (*embarrassed*): Here, here. Hold the umbrella, my dear, while I find my key. (AOUDA *obligingly holds the umbrella, while* FOGG *draws the key from his pocket.*)

AOUDA: What will you do now?

FOGG: Go on as before. (*Puts the key in the lock.*)

AOUDA: But Passepartout says you will be broken.

FOGG: Broken?

AOUDA: Passepartout says when one loses much money in English, they call it "broken."

FOGG: I see. Consider me broken in pounds, then, but never in spirit.

AOUDA: Me—I am broken in heart! Mr. Fogg, there is something I must tell you. I have for you—the rheumatic fever!

FOGG (*who has reclaimed his umbrella, now drops it upon the sidewalk*): Rheumatic— (*It is the first time we have seen him perturbed.*)

AOUDA: My heart goes bump-bump-bump. My cheeks are pink. My breath goes (*she gasps*)—like this.

FOGG: Rheumatic—

AOUDA: But this happens only when I am with you. Passepartout says—

FOGG: Rheumatic—

AOUDA: Passepartout says that this means I have the rheumatic fever for you.

(FOGG *picks up and closes the umbrella, ushers* AOUDA *into the house, seats her carefully upon the chair.*)

FOGG: You are sick.

AOUDA (*laughing*): No, no, not sick. I merely have the fever. Is that not the word? In French it is *amour*.

FOGG: I see. (*Picks up his umbrella, walks through the door, puts it over his head, and stands looking out across the audience.*)

AOUDA (*coming to the door*): What are you doing?

FOGG (*not turning and not changing his expression*): I am thinking.

AOUDA: About me?

FOGG: About you. (*A pause.*)

AOUDA: Do you like what you think?

FOGG: I am inclined to think that I like what I think. (*Another pause.*)

AOUDA: Have you decided yet?

FOGG (*still not turning*): Decided what?

AOUDA: Whatever it is you are trying to decide.

FOGG: I have decided.

AOUDA (*a catch in her voice*): What have you decided?

FOGG: That I must go to find Passepartout. He is loitering. (*Starts off.*)

AOUDA (*beginning to cry*): But what about me?

FOGG: Exactly why I must find Passepartout, my dear. He must go for the minister and make arrangements for us to be married tomorrow.

AOUDA (*happily*): Oh, Phileas!

FOGG: You are the second person to call me Phileas. Ralph is the other. (*Exits.*)

(AOUDA *claps her hands happily and runs to the carpetbag, from whence she draws her hats. Humming to herself, she tries first one and then the other, scattering them about the room and over the chair. As she does so, a commotion arises on the other side of the stage in front of the Reform Club. A number of people enter and gather before the door, whispering excitedly. We hear murmurs of, "He is here, I tell you." "Someone saw him at Charing Cross Railway not ten minutes ago." "Still carrying his umbrella." "Why isn't the band here yet?" The crowd grows larger. RALPH enters and hurries into the Club. He whispers something to the TWO GENTLEMEN. They put down their papers and begin to talk with him excitedly. The noise rises. A band begins to play off stage. Soon it marches down the street, playing loudly. Several little boys follow it, waving flags and banners. The band arrives in front of the Reform Club. More people enter. Cries of "Where is he?" "We want Phileas Fogg!" A great shout arises as FOGG appears, his umbrella over his head, drawn on by FIX and PASSEPARTOUT, who have his coattails. Behind them hurries the MINISTER.*)

PASSEPARTOUT (*rushing to the doorway of Number Seven*): Aouda! Aouda! Come quickly. We have won the wager.

AOUDA: Won! But—

PASSEPARTOUT: *Oui,* hurry, hurry. To the Reform Club!

AOUDA: But, my hat. Which hat?

PASSEPARTOUT: Women! (*He plunks a hat on her head at a rakish angle.*) There! Now come! (*Pulls* AOUDA *after him down the street.*

(FIX *pulls* FOGG. *The crowd roars again.*)

FOGG (*holding up his umbrella to the crowd*): Silence! (*Silence falls. To* FIX:) Release my coattails, sir! (FIX *lets go.*) Aouda, my dear, straighten your hat. (AOUDA *nervously adjusts her hat.*) We will now try to arrive at the bottom of this. (*To* PASSEPARTOUT:) You may explain.

PASSEPARTOUT: Well, sir, it was like this. You sent me into the rectory for the minister.

FOGG: I did.

PASSEPARTOUT: Well, when I got inside—

FIX (*excitedly*): When *we* got inside—

PASSEPARTOUT: Yes, when we got inside—

FOGG (*coolly*): When you got inside?

MINISTER: When they got inside—

FOGG: Let us begin once again. We arrived at Charing Cross Railway Station at nine P.M.

PASSEPARTOUT AND FIX (*giggling*): Correct.

FOGG: Correct. At nine-fifteen P.M. I sent you into the rectory to obtain the minister.

PASSEPARTOUT AND FIX (*giggling harder*): Correct.

FOGG: Correct. (*A pause.*) Well, continue.

PASSEPARTOUT AND FIX: When we got inside—

MINISTER: Yes, when they got inside—

FOGG: Yes?

MINISTER: I merely said I couldn't perform the marriage tomorrow, for tomorrow is a *Sunday,* and—

FOGG AND AOUDA: Sunday!

MINISTER: Yes, Sunday, and then these two picked me up and carried me forth onto the street.

FOGG: Sunday! My dear sir, you are quite incorrect. Tomorrow is Monday!

MINISTER (*hurt*): Mr. Fogg! You may argue that point with some ordinary person you meet on the street, but not with a minister! Do you think I have been preparing my sermon to speak in church on a Monday?

FOGG (*emphatically*): Tomorrow is Monday, the twenty-second of December!

MINISTER (*just as emphatically*): Tomorrow is Sunday, the twenty-first of December!

FOGG: We have gained a day!

PASSEPARTOUT AND FIX (*happily*): We have gained a day!

RALPH: But how?

FOGG: Of course. We traveled eastward toward the sun.

RALPH: Of course, of course.

FOGG: I should have thought of it before. Had we traveled westward we would have lost one. In a journey completely around the world, one must always gain or lose a day.

PASSEPARTOUT: And we gained one! You see, sir, providence is on our side.

AOUDA (*tapping* FOGG's *head*): Providence and a cool head.

RALPH (*with much feeling*): Phileas, my congratulations. You have done it. You have traversed the globe. You have gone around the world in eighty days! (*Shakes* FOGG's *hand enthusiastically*.)

(*The band strikes up. The people cheer.* FOGG *and* AOUDA *stand, shaking hands with their well-wishers.* FOGG *gives a sign to the* MINISTER, *whose voice we hear rising above the din: "Dearly beloved, we are gathered together—"*

THE CURTAIN FALLS.

OTHER PLAYS RECOMMENDED FOR
CHILDREN'S THEATER GROUPS

1. *Alice in Wonderland* by Lewis Carroll, adaptation by Charlotte B. Chorpenning; Dramatic Publishing Co., 1706 S. Prairie Ave., Chicago, 16, Illinois.

   Royalty—$10; Age span of actors—8th grade through high school; Cast requirements—18 characters and extras; Age span of audience—5th grade through high school; Playing time—2 hours.

2. *A Christmas Carol* by Charles Dickens, adaptation by Martha B. King; Children's Theater Press, "Cloverlot," Anchorage, Kentucky.

   Royalty—$15; Age span of actors—8th through 10th grades; Cast requirements—7 "women," 11 "men," 5 children, 3 ghosts; Age span of audience—4th through 10th grades; Playing time—1½ hours.

3. *The Christmas Nightingale* by Eric P. Kelly, dramatized by Phyllis N. Groff; Children's Theater Press, "Cloverlot," Anchorage, Kentucky.

   Royalty—$15; Age span of actors—8th through 10th grades; Cast requirements—3 "women," 6 "men," 4 children, extras; Age span of audience—4th through 10th grades; Playing time—1½ hours.

4. *Cinderella,* adaptation by Herman Ould; Baker's Plays, 569 Boylston St., Boston 16, Mass.

   Royalty—$5; Age span of actors—5th through 8th grades; Cast requirements—17 speaking parts and extras; Age span of audience—2nd through 8th grades; Playing time—30 minutes.

149

5. *The Clown Who Ran Away* by Conrad Seiler; Longman's Green and Co., 55 Fifth Ave., New York 3, N.Y.

   Royalty—$15; Age span of actors—5th through 8th grades; Cast requirements—22 parts; Age span of audience—2nd through 8th grades; Playing time—1½ hours.

6. *The Dyspeptic Ogre* by Percival Wilde; Baker's Plays, 569 Boylston St., Boston 16, Mass.

   Royalty—$10; Age span of actors—5th through 8th grades; Cast requirements—2 "men," 1 "woman," 14 or more children; Age span of audience—2nd through 8th grades; Playing time—40 minutes.

7. *Hansel and Gretel,* adaptation by Madge Miller; Children's Theater Press, "Cloverlot," Anchorage, Kentucky.

   Royalty—$15; Age span of actors—7th through 9th grades; Cast requirements—3 "women," 1 "man," 1 girl, 1 boy, 1 cat, extras; Age span of audience—2nd through 9th grades; Playing time—2 hours.

8. *Snow White and the Seven Dwarfs,* adaptation by Jessie Braham White; Samuel French, 25 West 45th St., New York 19, N.Y.

   Royalty—$25; Age span of actors—5th through 8th grades; Cast requirements—24 characters; Age span of audience— 2nd through 8th grades; Playing time—1½ hours.

HELPFUL BOOKS FOR THE TEACHER OR CHILDREN'S THEATER DIRECTOR

1. *Arts in the Classroom* by Natalie Robinson Cole, John Day Company, New York, N.Y. An inspiration to any teacher, this book abounds in ideas for creative techniques.

2. *Stagecraft for Amateurs* by F. A. Marteau and John Holgates, Baker's Plays, 569 Boylston St., Boston 16, Mass. This book covers basic staging requirements.

3. *Theater for Children* by Winifred Ward, Children's Theater Press, "Cloverlot," Anchorage, Kentucky. This book covers costuming, staging, advertising, and financing.